WISCONSIN
LEGENDS & LORE

WISCONSIN
LEGENDS & LORE

TEA KRULOS

THE
History
PRESS

Published by The History Press
Charleston, SC
www.historypress.com

First published 2020

Manufactured in the United States

ISBN 9781467143448

Library of Congress Control Number: 2020934450

Notice: The information in this book is true and complete to the best of our knowledge. It is offered without guarantee on the part of the author or The History Press. The author and The History Press disclaim all liability in connection with the use of this book.

Dedicated to Megan, Margot and Rita

CONTENTS

ACKNOWLEDGEMENTS

One of the great things about organizing the Milwaukee Paranormal Conference and working on previous books like *Monster Hunters* is that I've gotten a chance to meet all the experts who greatly informed the stories I share in this book. Research from these great people helped shape parts of this book: Linda S. Godfrey, Allison Jornlin, J. Nathan Couch, Jay Bachochin, Scott Markus, Larry and Jen Dopke, Noah Leigh and the Paranormal Investigators of Milwaukee, Loren Coleman, Tobias and Emily Wayland, Lisa van Buskirk, Wendy Staats, Mike Huberty, American Ghost Walks, Charlie Hintz (Cult of Weird), Valerie Kedrowski, Chad Lewis, Anna Lardinois and my friends at the Old Baraboo Inn.

The following people aren't in the paranormal field but were helpful to me nonetheless: Janice Christensen, Lee Gutowski (*Riverwest Currents*), Dave Luhrssen and John Schneider (of the *Shepherd Express*), Matt Wild (of the *Milwaukee Record*), Naomi Shertsy (Moonlight Retreat), Risto Pakarinen and Kathy Nichols. Special thanks to John Rodrigue, who was my guide and acquisitions editor at The History Press.

I'd also like to thank my supportive family and, of course, my dear Kate, who has traveled many a strange road with me.

Thank you all for being weird.

INTRODUCTION

WISCONSIN

GOOD LAND OF STORIES

Wisconsin is a state filled with a diverse legacy of storytellers. This land's earliest Native American storytellers told of how the earth came to be in their creation tales and the adventures of the spirit entity Winnebozho and how recognizable terrain, landmarks and members of the animal kingdom came about.

The word *Wisconsin* evolved from the Algonquian word *Meskonsing* or *Meskousing*, with different interpretations saying the word refers to the Wisconsin River or the redstone banks along it. Jean Nicolet was probably the first European to visit the land that would become Wisconsin when he traveled the Great Lakes in 1634. Explorer Jacques Marquette was the first European to reach the Wisconsin River, noting the name Meskousing in his journal. French speakers changed this word to *Ouisconsin*, and eventually it was anglicized to "Wisconsin."

Over the next hundred years, visitors here were mainly French fur trappers. After the War of 1812, the land that would be Wisconsin's industry switched from fur trading to mining, and some early lore got us the nickname of the "Badger State"—not from a surplus badger population but rather from miners who took shelter in holes that they ("the badgers") dug.

Wisconsin became a state in 1848, with the lumber industry being a part of economic growth in the northern forests. We got the nickname "America's Dairyland" because of our growing agricultural industry. Today, a ride on the country roads of Wisconsin will lead you through cornfields and past faded red barns and herds of cattle.

INTRODUCTION

Wisconsin's melting pot of Native American and European produced stories told in lumberjack camps and mines, under circus tents, in fishing boats and in breweries, from campfires to bar stools; they were eventually recorded in written word. We've had quite a history in this state of remarkable, innovative and even infamous people, from legendary lumberjacks to notorious gangsters. Wisconsin bred the industry of the beer barons, the Ringling Bros. (and many other circuses) and Harley-Davidson. Wisconsin is essential to story writers everywhere, as its largest city, Milwaukee, was home to Christopher Latham Sholes, who developed an early version of the typewriter.

Wisconsin has been home to many brilliant minds and creative people over the years, including writers August Derleth, Zona Gale, Thornton Wilder, Laura Ingalls Wilder (Thornton and Laura weren't related to each other or to another famous Wisconsinite, comedian Gene Wilder) and Robert Bloch, all of whom contributed significantly to their genres. Contemporary writers who have called Wisconsin home include successful authors Peter Straub, Patrick Rothfuss and Neil Gaiman. Kareem Abdul-Jabbar, basketball star turned novelist, lived here and brought fame to the Milwaukee Bucks, and the state continues to produce talented writers, musicians and artists.

One of our most legendary residents was born Erik Weisz but is better known by his stage name, Harry Houdini. Originally from Hungary but spending his formative years in Milwaukee and Appleton in the 1880s, Houdini's magic illusions and death-defying escape acts led some to believe that he had actual magic powers, and his death on Halloween 1926 adds to his mysterious life story.

This book has been a thrill for me to work on, as some of the stories within are ones I heard as a boy around the campfire and later read in books and newspaper articles. As a chronicler of weird things, I've kept tabs on stories of legends and lore. For my work as the director of the annual Milwaukee Paranormal Conference, I've hosted a panel on Wisconsin urban legends and have established a vast network of researchers who look to investigate stories of the supernatural and sometimes come face to face with it in the process.

A NOTE ON THE chapters: Quite a few of our Wisconsin stories could fall into more than one category, so I've organized them under the headings that made the most sense to me. Here, then, is a collection of stories from throughout the state. Some have been entertaining or frightening generations of Wisconsinites, and some are more recent entries. This is not a complete compendium of every piece of Wisconsin lore, but I've rounded up some of our most famous stories along with lesser-known tales. I hope you enjoy these legends and pass them on as people have done here for hundreds of years. Help keep Wisconsin folklore alive. Let's keep these stories moving. To quote our state motto: "Forward!"

PART I

NATIVE AMERICAN LEGENDS

I t is important to remember that before European colonizers arrived in Wisconsin, these lands belonged to native tribes. The Algonquin people are a widespread group of Native Americans in North America who share a similar language but come from many different tribes. Algonquin tribes include the Ojibwes, Salteaux, Crees, Naskapis and Innus, among others, all of whom lived throughout the northern forests of the Atlantic and the Great Lakes regions of the United States and Canada. Today, Wisconsin is home to Chippewa, Potawatomi, Menominee, Ho-Chunk, Oneida, Ojibwe, Mohican and Brothertown nations and tribal communities.

The names of many lands, lakes and rivers we use originated from native languages. Native storytelling is rich with tales of how natural features in Wisconsin, such as lakes and mountains, were formed, as well as powerful, whimsical or frightening entities that roam the land. Native stories find people in harmony with the animal kingdom and nature as a whole.

CREATION STORIES

Each native tribe of Wisconsin has its own stories chronicling how the earth was formed, varying among the tribes, but the similarities and recurring themes are apparent. The Menominee creation story says that Manabozho was born from a woman, Wenonah, and a spirit father, the North Wind. Manabozho is a frequent figure in creation stories, and other tribes know him as Waynaboozhoo, Winnebozho and other variations. He's described as being a predecessor to man (sometimes called the "original man"), a spirit entity that is not good or evil and is sometimes described as a trickster spirit.

The Ojibwe earth origin story says that a new earth was created after the world was covered by a great flood. Waynaboozhoo and a group of animals managed to save themselves by floating on a log. Waynaboozhoo tells the animals that one of them must swim to the bottom of the water, grab a bit of dirt and bring it to the surface to create a new earth. Several animals—Loon, Mink, Otter and others—attempt the dive but can't swim deep enough. Muskrat finally gets the job done, grabbing a paw full of earth (but dying in the process). The new earth was placed on Turtle's back, and as all four winds blew, the land grew bigger and bigger, forming an island. Waynaboozhoo and the animals began to dance in a circle around the island, a ceremonial dance that is still performed today.

The Potawatomi creation story is similar, with Wi' saka, the Great Spirit, floating in a canoe with no land in sight. Muskrat and other aquatic animals help him out by bringing him handfuls of earth, which he slowly molded into ground. Other tribes have a similar tale, including Sky Woman planting and creating a new world after the flood. Other stories tell how things like seasons, weather, terrain and unique animal features came to be.

The Ojibwe story "Fisher Goes to the Sky World" explains how the four seasons were created. In the legend, four animal friends—Fisher, Lynx, Otter and Wolverine—try to steal the sun by digging a hole to Sky World. By the time the Sky People discover the group, they have made a hole big enough to warm the Earth for part of the year.

A Menominee story told in the book *Wisconsin Indian Literature: Anthology of Native Voices* explains how the first tribal clans—Bear and Eagle— originated: "Macq-Awaetok [Great Spirit] made the Sun, the stars, and the Earth. Mother Earth gave birth to Keso (the Moon)." The Moon gave birth to twins who finished creating the world, lands and lakes, animals and plants. A great bear with a copper tail arose from the banks of the Menominee River, and the Great Spirit transformed him into a person, the first Menominee. He was soon joined by an eagle, who also turned into a human and became his brother. Bear and Eagle formed the tribe's

Native American family in Odanah, Wisconsin (Ashland County), circa 1930–40. *Wisconsin Historical Society, image 52836.*

groups or clans. The new Menominee chiefs descended from Bear clan, and the warriors came out of Eagle clan.

Eagle and Bear were soon joined by Beaver, Sturgeon, Elk, Crane, Wolf, Dog and Deer, all of whom were also transformed into humans and formed clans.

Native stories also tell us how lakes, mountains and other parts of Wisconsin's landscape were formed. A Ho-Chunk story about how Lake Winnebago was created says that Ho-Chunk spirit entity Wak' djunk' aga (another variant of Winnebozho) wanted to speak to Ma-ona (the Creator) and asked Bear how he can visit him. Bear told him that the only way to see Ma-ona is to die, so Wak' djunk' aga went to a village and asked the warriors there to shoot him with their arrows. They complied, but the arrows couldn't kill the spirit entity, which greatly saddened Wak' djunk' aga. He walked up a cliff and cried so many tears that Lake Winnebago was created.

Thunder Mountain, in Marinette County, is said by Potawatomi and Menominee natives to be a nesting place for mythical Thunderbirds or Thunderers, giant eagle-like birds. A pond on the mountain was home to a horned water serpent that battled the Thunderbirds. A Potawatomi legend has it that a hunter encountered a Thunderbird fighting the water serpent. Both entities asked the hunter to intervene. Closing his eyes and letting an arrow fly, the hunter hit the Thunderbird, imprisoning it in the mountain. Other places the giant birds were said to roost were the mountain ranges of the Penokee Iron Range near Hurley in Iron County and Fox Bluff on the north shore of Lake Mendota in Madison.

Another story of Thunderbirds comes from Sturgeon Bay and also involves them battling a water serpent. This one says that a few Menominee girls were swimming in the bay when a giant water snake captured them and took them to its underwater den. The girls' father asks for help from Manabus, fasting and praying for six days until Manabus appeared to him in a dream and told him that he would help. Manabus summoned Thunderbirds, found the girls and rescued them.

Spirit Island, located in the St. Louis River near Superior, is said to have a Romeo and Juliet–style romance story. A young Chippewa woman and a Sioux man, daughter and son of two rival chiefs, were in love with each other. The woman saved her lover from a battle, and they fled by night to the island in a canoe. The daughter's angry father pursued them, but at the island, he only found their canoe and a smoldering campfire. The couple had disappeared entirely except for their pairs of side-by-side moccasins left behind, having been taken to another realm by a love spirit. It has been said that love songs sung by their spirits could be heard to those visiting the island at night.

Many stories exist that explain how the features of animals came to be. In the Potawatomi story "How Mko Lost His Tail," Mko (Bear) is tricked by Fox to icefish with his long tail, which is bitten off by the fish he is trying to catch.

In the Ho-Chunk story "The Fox and the Grease Kettle," an animal council meets, a kettle of fat placed in the middle of them, to determine which animals will get the most fat on their bodies, to give them warmth. The wily Fox decides to skip the vote and jumps into the kettle, emerging extremely fat, but the animals, led by Bear, grab him and squeeze the fat out of him, except a little above the legs. He was kicked out of the council for his trickery and remained a sly and slender animal.

The Ojibwe story of the "Lac Courte Oreilles Frog" says that a man was about to shoot a big frog with a bow and arrow so that he and his hungry family could have something to eat. The frog, in an effort to save his own life, told the man that he would be rewarded if he was allowed to go free. Early the next morning, the man heard a chorus of bullfrogs chirping, and returning to the pond, he found it flush with spawning walleye. This fable led to the belief that when you hear frogs croaking in the spring, it's a signal that you'll find spawning walleye.

RED HORN

One of the earliest figures of Wisconsin folklore is Red Horn, an ancient Ho-Chunk hero who wore human heads as earrings and had long, red hair fashioned into a point. He was also known as "He Who Wears Human Heads as Earrings," and his unusual jewelry could speak. Red Horn was one of the five sons of Earthmaker, and the stories about him are known as the Red Horn Cycle. In these adventures, Red Horn challenges giants and water spirits and leads battles against evil entities.

The Gottschall Rockshelter pictographs in a cave in Muscoda, Wisconsin, are located in the southwestern part of the state and were painted around AD 900–1000. This art depicts the story of Red Horn and the Giants.

Another story about Red Horn has him winning a tribal chief's daughter's hand in marriage after a race between his brothers and Turtle and other

Native American at Red Cliff Reservation, Bayfield County, 1913. *Wisconsin Historical Society, image 52830.*

members of the animal kingdom (he declined the wedding, as he was too young, choosing later to marry She Who Wears White Beaver Skin). In another story, Red Horn and his crew played an epic game of ball with giants and defeated them.

MAKIA′ WISAG: THE LITTLE PEOPLE

Many cultures have stories of mischievous groups of small people who will play tricks, ranging from humorous to malicious if they are not appeased—a famous example would be the leprechauns of Ireland.

The Brothertown tell of a race of little people called the Makia' wisag, who would stop at peoples' houses asking for things to eat or small favors. If they were not given what they asked for, they would point at the person, which would make him or her turn invisible, and the Makia' wisag would sneak into the home and take whatever they wanted.

FRIGHTENING ENTITIES

Menominee legend tells of Mashenomak, a giant sturgeon-like fish monster, that would drag fishers down into lakes and devour them. The Menominees asked Manabush to help them defeat the beast, and he agreed. He floated out on the lake on a raft, singing and inviting Mashenomak to eat him. When the giant fish devoured him, he found that his brothers Bear, Deer, Porcupine, Raven and Squirrel were all prisoners inside the massive belly. They all began to sing a war song and dance, and Manabush killed Mashenomak by stabbing him in his heart three times. Manabush then cut a hole in his side, and he and his animal brethren escaped.

Probably the most frightening entities of Algonquin legend are the Windigo, sometimes spelled Wendigo, Wiindigo, Wee-tee-ko and other variations. Similar beings in other stories are called atchen, atuush or chenoo.

The Windigo stories are found in Algonquin legends throughout the Midwest and Canada. Symbolic of the harshness of winter, a Windigo is said to be cursed with an overpowering hunger for human flesh.

Winter could mean famine, starvation or freezing to death. A sudden cold and howling wind is associated with starvation and cannibalism. Much

Ojibwe women dressed up for a celebration of the return of Native Americans soldiers from World War I. Town of Reserve, Sawyer County, Wisconsin, 1919. *Wisconsin Historical Society, image 23767.*

as the name differs, so does the exact representation of the Windigo. It is sometimes depicted as a giant, lumbering creature fifteen feet or taller with an elk skull for a head. Other versions say the Windigo is more of an evil spirit that possesses a person and puts him or her into a decaying, zombie-like state. Some say shamans send the Windigo as a curse. In most versions, the Windigo has a frozen, icy heart, an emaciated appearance and a constant hunger for human flesh.

There is a special ceremony during times of famine in which tribe members would wear masks and dance backward around a drum to ward away the Windigo. You can still find places like Lake Windigo on Star Island in Minnesota that are named after the creature.

Another entity you don't want to encounter in a winter forest is Ah-ne-pe, a ferocious great gray spirit wolf and namesake of the Ahnapee River in Kewaunee County. Potawatomi chief Katoose told the story that the great gray wolf, which he said was like "an evil spirit," stalked those lands, killing tribe members.

"There were many wolves in those days, but none like the big grey wolf *An-ne-pe*. He fed upon women and children. If a [Potawatomi] girl strayed into the forest when we made our camps here, she never returned. If a child played in these bushes when we came to this river, he never more came back to his mother. Even our hunters sometimes came staggering back into camp with their clothing torn and the blood running from red wounds," Chief Katoose is quoted as saying in a December 8, 1923 article in the *Kewaunee County Press*.

Another dark force is what the Ojibwes called "Bear Walkers," said to be evil sorcerers who walk at night in the form of bears. They could use their powers to hurt or kill people. A fireball or flashing light was said to indicate their presence.

PART II

LUMBERJACK LORE AND CLASSIC TALL TALES

Classic Wisconsin folklore came from the rugged beginnings of the state—the great outdoors, the farmland, the vast forests of the north, the Kettle Moraine and Lake Michigan (and Lake Superior to the north). Wisconsin's beginnings revolved around the lumber, agriculture and dairy industries. Lumberjacks and raftsmen, farmers and fishers entertained themselves with tall tales and big fish stories at work and in saloons.

Two prominent figures in the recording of classic Wisconsin folklore were Charles E. Brown (1872–1946), a curator at the State History Society of Wisconsin and the secretary of the Wisconsin Archaeological Society, and his wife, Dorothy Moulding Brown (1896–1983). Charles first worked as an attendant at the Milwaukee Public Museum before he became the first director of the Wisconsin Historical Society's museum in Madison, a position he held from 1908 to 1944. In 1913, he began teaching a folklore program during the University of Wisconsin–Madison's summer session.

Charles met Dorothy when she was hired to assist him in 1935 with the Federal Writers' Project (they married in 1937), a program developed by the Roosevelt administration as part of its Works Progress Administration, which, among other things, allocated money in each state for authors and researchers to collect folklore and stories. Charles and Dorothy led the Wisconsin Federal Writers' Project, which ran during the Depression from 1935 to 1938, but the program was terminated in 1939. Still, in the time they did have, the project recorded more than six hundred field interviews with Wisconsin residents and researched old newspaper articles, obscure books and other sources, documenting stories, songs, traditions and superstitions.

After the program ended, the Browns continued their work, running the Wisconsin Folklore Society from 1940 to 1947. The stories they collected were sometimes published in small booklets. These little books explored stories of Paul Bunyan, buried treasure, native legends, ghosts and other local tales. Many of the stories retold in this chapter are sourced from these booklets compiled by the Browns directly or from publications that use them as a reference. You can find PDF files of scans of the original publications on the Wisconsin Historical Society's website. Following are some of these stories of early Wisconsin lore.

PAUL BUNYAN

The most famous piece of classic folklore from Wisconsin is the larger-than-life Paul Bunyan, a giant bearded lumberjack, carrying a huge axe over his shoulder, accompanied by his mighty companion, Babe, the Blue Ox.

In his book *Out of the Northwoods: The Many Lives of Paul Bunyan*, author Michael Edmonds includes an appendix of "Bunyan Tales Told in Wisconsin, 1885–1915." One of the stories includes this description:

> *Bunyan was a powerful giant, seven feet tall and with a stride of seven feet. He was famous throughout the lumbering districts for his physical strength and for the ingenuity with which he met difficult situations. He was so powerful that no man could successfully oppose him, and his ability to get drunk was proverbial. So great was his lung capacity that he called his men to dinner by blowing through a hollow tree a blast so strong that it blew down the timber on a tract of sixty acres, and when he spoke, the limbs sometimes fell from trees.*

Additional details include that he would smoke a pipe that held "about a bushel of tobacco" in it and that trimming his beard required two skilled men with axes.

Paul Bunyan tales spread from Maine and Ontario across the northern forests to the Pacific Northwest. For decades, they remained deep in the woods in lumber camps, but eventually, oral tradition made its way to print and mass consumption. Maine, Michigan, Minnesota and California all have made a claim to be the birthplace of Paul Bunyan, but as Edmonds explained in *Out of the Northwoods*, "Wisconsin timber cruiser Bill Mulhollen told the first reliably documented tales of Paul Bunyan during the winter of 1885–1886 in the upper Wisconsin River Valley, at a logging camp a few miles north of Tomahawk, Wisconsin," and thus, "Wisconsin has the best claim of any state to being Paul Bunyan's birthplace."

Another early Bunyan storyteller was Gene Shepard, a well-known land surveyor, prankster and storyteller of the Rhinelander area. Shepard said that he was the originator of the Paul Bunyan stories. Even if this claim isn't valid, he was among the earliest of the people to have shared the legends of the mighty lumberjack.

It's unknown what the inspiration for the Bunyan stories might have been initially. Bunyan might have been an actual taller-than-average lumberjack, or the stories might have been derivative of French folklore, passed down by loggers who originate from France.

In some cases, lumberjack stories with different twists were now retold, starring Bunyan and his crew. Bunyan's legendary status is due to a mix of elements from various sources. Bunyan stories were passed around by oral tradition—lumberjacks entertained themselves by singing, dancing and telling tall tales. "If the men gathered for entertainment, each one in the outfit was required to do his part; he must sing a song, tell a tale, whistle, or dance; failing to do so, he was required to donate a pound of tobacco to the 'poor-box,'" prolific Wisconsin author August Derleth wrote in his book *The Wisconsin: River of a Thousand Isles*, first published in 1942.

When stories weren't being told, the lumberjacks sang songs like "The Little Brown Bulls" and "The Shanty Boy on the Big Eau Claire."

Bunyan stories first appeared in print and reached a mass audience in 1910 in a Milwaukee-based nature magazine called *Outer's Book*. In 1914, classic bits of Bunyan lore were created and spread by the Red River Lumber Company, which printed and distributed pamphlets that included retellings of Bunyan stories by the company's advertising manager, William Laughead. These advertisements were where many of Paul's supporting cast got their names, including his giant ox, Babe, who had turned blue from the winter chill. Other supporting characters in Bunyan's lumber camp included lumberjack Big Ola, bookkeeper Johnny Inkslinger and the camp cook, Sourdough Sam.

Bunyan's right-hand man was Brimstone Bill, "a tough, burly man with a florid complexion and a full, white beard" who "held the national record for

Loggers posing on the railroad tracks by Saddle Mound in Jackson County, 1896. *Wisconsin Historical Society, WHS-1964.*

profanity. No one has surpassed him since. He could still burn the bark off a big spruce tree with his flow of lurid language."

Collections of classic stories told by lumberjacks, as well as new creations by fiction writers, began to appear in newspapers, magazines and books as part of the "Bunyan craze" in the 1920s. Charles E. Brown, of the Wisconsin Folklore Society, was also an enthusiastic collector of Bunyan stories, interviewing lumberjacks from around Wisconsin and publishing booklets of the stories that he recorded. After his death, his wife, Dorothy Moulding Brown, collected these stories in a book titled *What Say You of Paul?*, published in 1947.

There are more than one hundred recorded Bunyan stories, many of which take place at the lumberjack's Big Onion River camp or deal with their attempts to lumber the area by the fictional Round River. "Most of the exploits of Paul Bunyan center at Round River. Here Bunyan and his crew labored all one winter to clear the pine from a single forty," James P. Leary wrote in his book *Wisconsin Folklore*, referring to a forty-acre plot of forest. "This was a most peculiar forty in that it was shaped like a pyramid with a heavy timber growth on all sides."

The story goes that Paul Bunyan and crew cleared 1 million feet of pine and in spring started moving it down the river toward the sawmill, but it was "not until they passed their old camp several times that they realized that the river was round and had no outlet whatever."

Some of the most common types of Bunyan tales include amazing feats of his strength, his crew's battle with extreme weather, creating geography (Bunyan creating valleys by dragging his axe on the ground, for example), encounters with strange animals and the incredible amount of food and drink Bunyan's camp consumed.

A well-known Paul Bunyan tale relates how his breakfast skillet for making pancakes was so big that his men skated around on it with hams on their feet to grease it. Another tale tells how a lake was transformed into a giant vat of pea soup that fed the entire lumber camp.

As the stories left the camp and proliferated, they lost some of their rough edges, polished by magazine writers instead of lumberjacks around a campfire. Eventually, the stories became geared more toward children, with Walt Disney Studios creating a popular short animated film titled *Paul Bunyan* in 1958. You can still spot the giant lumberjack and his ox in Wisconsin and around the Midwest, promoting a range of things from campgrounds to pancake houses.

A Paul Bunyan statue outside the Paul Bunyan's Cook Shanty restaurant in Wisconsin Dells. *Mike Huberty*.

Paul Bunyan is not the only legendary strongman in Wisconsin lore. Other regional versions of similar tall tales can be found in the state. Albert Gamroth, aka Gamroth the Strong, was a Silesian (a region of Poland, Germany and the former Czechoslovakia) who led a band of Polish immigrants to Trempealeau County in western Wisconsin in the 1850s.

Gamroth is said to have been slow of movement and speech but was a kind and helpful man and incredibly powerful. Typical stories describe his acts of strength—picking up a telephone pole and moving it by himself, hauling a broken-down wagon full of bricks, carrying fifteen or sixteen sacks of grain on his back and even running an entire twelve-by-sixteen-foot granary across the street. He often saw groups of men struggling with a task and would say his catchphrase, "*Co chcecie, chlopey? Jo wom pokozo*," or "What do you want, boys? Let me show you how it's done." If Gamroth saw men fighting, he would pick them both up by their collars and knock their heads together.

A rougher version of Paul Bunyan was said to be a character named Whiskey Jack, a raftsman, one of the people who transported lumber and other goods down the rivers. Whiskey Jack, who was also said to be seven feet tall, was the toughest of a tough group who seemed to like drinking and fighting as their favored pastimes. August Derleth wrote on the legacy of the raftsmen in his book *The Wisconsin: River of a Thousand Isles*: "For brawling, the raftsmen were indistinguishable from the lumberjacks; they brawled all the way down the Wisconsin—from Wasau to Kilbourn, from Portage to Sauk City, from Lone Rock to Prairie du Chien. They were rough, rugged men, lusty in living, filled with gusto, addicted to Booze, Bawds* [an archaic term for someone who runs or works in a brothel], and Battle."

STRANGE CRITTERS

Many tales shared at lumberjack camps told stories of unusually large or weird animals that lurked in the woods. The stories were sometimes spun to get a scare out of gullible new lumberjacks who would lie in their bunks awake and think about the stories they had been told of strange creatures creeping through the dark forests.

A classic Paul Bunyan legend tells of chipmunks that ate discarded prune stones that made them grow to be as big as bears. In another, Bunyan and his crew had the poorly conceived idea of combatting giant mosquitos

Lumberjacks in a bunkhouse at Ole Emerson's lumber camp, Bayfield County, 1904. *Wisconsin Historical Society, WHS-83371.*

by introducing giant bees to the forest, which led to hideous and gigantic mosquito-bee hybrids that would bite and sting the lumberjacks from both ends of their bodies.

The sidehill gouger was a strange and ferocious feline that had one small pair of legs and one long pair to adapt to life walking on the hill of the pyramid-shaped forty acres at the Round River. Other comically odd critters included snow snakes, the axe-shaped Axehandle Hound, an ape-like creature called the Agropelter (which threw rocks at lumberjacks), the Goofus Bird, Rumptifusel (a hideous, hairy monster that looked like a fur coat that would eat lumberjacks) and the Teakettler (a stout dog that could whistle loudly), all of which looked like creatures that might have stepped out of *Alice's Adventures in Wonderland*. In the lakes and rivers, lumberjacks would struggle with the bizarre Cougar Fish, Log Gar, Upland Trout and Whirligig Fish.

WISCONSIN: MOTHER OF CIRCUSES

One of the most colorful aspects of Wisconsin history is its tie to the circus. The "big top" business started in New York but moved west to Wisconsin, which became known as the "Mother of Circuses" and the home base and winter headquarters for more than one hundred different circuses during the golden age of the big top. The terrain was filled with traveling troupes of clowns, acrobats, exotic animals and other performers.

The most famous were the Ringling Bros. and the Barnum & Bailey circuses. Barnum & Bailey set up headquarters in Delavan, Wisconsin, after its beginnings in 1871. The small town would become home to twenty more circuses. In 1884, the Ringling Bros., originally from Iowa, moved from Prairie du Chien to Baraboo and set up headquarters (it bought the Barnum & Bailey Circus in 1907, and the two acts combined in 1919). Baraboo, known as "Circus City," was also home to the Gollmar Bros. Circus, John Robinson's Circus, Hodgini Brothers Combined Railroad Shows and others.

The Ringlings gave their first show on a street corner of Baraboo on May 19, 1884. Their company started with nine wagons, a main tent, a sideshow tent and a troupe of about twenty performers, although it would rapidly expand. The Ringlings were performers themselves—Al Ringling's act, for example, included juggling and rolling cannonballs around his arms and neck.

Janesville, Whitewater, Watertown and Evansville were also circus towns. In addition to the performers, large numbers of Wisconsinites were hired to build wagons and tents, sew costumes, tend to animals and do other work.

One of Ringling's biggest stars was Lillian Leitzel, the "world's greatest aerialist," according to *Wisconsin Circus Lore, 1850–1908: Stories of the Big Top, Sawdust Ring, Menagerie, and Sideshows*, compiled by Dorothy Moulding Brown and published in 1947. Leitzel, born in Germany, was a headlining star after the Ringling Bros. and Barnum & Bailey circuses merged, but she died in a tragic accident when her trapeze ropes broke during a performance in 1931.

Brown also documents circus lore about famous characters like "Colonel" George Washington Hall, aka "Popcorn George," who was married to a snake charmer who performed under the name Zula Zangara. Hall ran his circus from Evansville, keeping many exotic animals in his home. Hall caused a fright in Evansville on occasions

Ringling Bros. and Barnum & Bailey Circus star Lillian Leitzel, performing in 1930, one year before she fell to her death. *Circus World Museum.*

when his leopard, alligator and twenty-three-foot python escaped from his show. Other entertaining circus performers included Captain Sigby, who trained horses for the Seibel Brothers Circus (based in Watertown) and Zazel the Human Bullet, who was fired from a cannon to the top of the circus tent, where she grabbed a trapeze at the Ringling Bros. and Barnum & Bailey Circus in the 1880s.

Animals were as big a star attraction as human performers, and Wisconsin was home to famous elephants Romeo, of the Mable Bros. Circus of Delavan, and Big Charlie, sold by Ringling Bros to Colonel George Hall's circus. Other animals found throughout the circus towns included lions, tigers, camels, apes and bears.

Over the years, the many circuses that had called Wisconsin home dwindled and disappeared until only Ringling Bros. and Barnum & Bailey Circus remained (although it moved to Florida). Weakening attendance, animal rights protests and a high operating cost finally caught up with the "Greatest Show on Earth," which had its final performance on May 21, 2017, in New York.

In Baraboo, you can see displays related to Wisconsin's circus history at the Circus World Museum, which is set up on the site of Ringling Bros.' former winter headquarters complex.

THE FIGHTING FINCHES

Certain families live on in notoriety. In the pre–Civil War era, from the 1830s to the 1860s, the Finches, a family of bandits, terrorized south-central Wisconsin in Rock and Jefferson Counties, stealing cattle and horses and taking refuge in a hideout in a swamp near Lake Mills, as explored by a 1937 booklet titled *The Fighting Finches: Tales of Freebooters of the Pioneer Countryside in Rock and Jefferson Counties*, compiled by Dorothy Moulding Brown for the Federal Writers' Project.

The "Fighting Finches," as they were known, came from Michigan. Sometimes said to be a family of twelve, their exploits included stealing livestock with lassos, and their name became synonymous with thievery. Settler children were told not to "finch" something that wasn't theirs. Jack Finch had "great strength" and was "widely known to be a rough and tumble wrestler in days when every county had its champion," according to Brown's booklet, which also says that Patsy Finch was "was reputed to have been one of the most attractive among the beautiful Finch women. She was, like others of her female relatives, a very skillful and fearless horsewoman and could ride bareback as well as in the saddle. She had flashing blue-black eyes and long black hair, which streamed out behind her as she traveled down the road on some errand."

Patsy, as the story goes, left her rambunctious family behind and married a wealthy merchant in Milwaukee:

> They were a hard-drinking, hard-fisted, and hard-riding crew. Mounted on fast horses, they descended on the prairie and woodland farms, driving before them the farmers' horses and cattle. They were expert shots with pistol and rifle, but so far as it is known, they never committed a murder. One of their hideouts is said to have been in the big Rock Lake, or London Swamp....There on an island, a high spot in the swampy fastness, they were secure after a raid or when too hard-hunted.

When the Finches rode out of their swamp hideout and hit the road, "honest folks would shiver and honest folks' dogs would howl" when they stormed through town. The Finches are said to have hidden treasure in Lake Mills, Fort Atkinson and on the shores of Lake Koshkonong.

Wisconsin got a break from the Finches' reign during the gold rush, when it's said many of the clan headed west. The family's notorious escapades stopped after the Civil War, but their legend lives on.

ROARING DAN SEAVEY

We usually think of pirates as raiders of the Atlantic Ocean, but "Roaring Dan" Seavey plundered the Great Lakes. Seavey moved from Portland, Maine, to Marinette, Wisconsin, in the late 1880s, where he married and had children. The Seavey family moved to Milwaukee, where Dan worked as a fisher, farmer and saloon owner. In 1898, he left his family and headed west, hoping to become rich in the gold rush. Seavey wasn't successful and returned to the Midwest, buying a schooner he named *The Wanderer* in Escanaba, Michigan. He began pirating cargo from other ships, sex trafficking and poaching venison. One of his more famous exploits was stealing the schooner *Nellie Johnson* in Grand Haven, Michigan. Seavey got the entire crew intoxicated and pushed them overboard, after which he absconded with the ship and headed to Chicago, where he sold the ship's cargo.

Toward the end of his career, Seavey, perhaps sick of a life of crime, switched sides and worked for the U.S. Marshals Service, where he fought against his former trades of smuggling, poaching and piracy. Seavey retired to Peshtigo, Wisconsin, in the 1920s and died there in 1949. Milwaukee's Great Lakes Distillery pays tribute to him with its Roaring Dan's Rum.

BURIED TREASURE

There are several legends of buried treasure hidden throughout Wisconsin. Sometimes hidden stashes of loot have been stumbled upon, but others are tall tales that have lived on through the decades. Bluffs are places that seem to easily draw lore, whether it's stories of lovers leaping to their deaths or hidden secrets. The most famous treasure story is the legend of Bogus Bluff, located on the Wisconsin River, about fifty miles west of Madison. It towers 220 feet above Highway 60, and tales of hidden treasure there date back to 1850.

"Standing out like a sentinel on the Wisconsin River in Richland County is a tall hill, its sides scarred, rough and craggy. This is the famous Bogus Bluff, once the home of a den of counterfeiters," a *Wisconsin State Journal* report in 1923 reads.

By that time, the legend of Bogus Bluff had been handed down for a few generations—the story of a stash in the bluff of "French coins, Spanish doubloons and good American dollars, placed there in the days when the

Wisconsin valley was an outpost of civilization and travelers were at the mercy of Indian war parties and river pirates." A trading post in Prairie du Chien that was robbed is said to be the origin of the treasure.

During the Civil War, a gang of counterfeiters set up shop in the bluff. The story goes that government officials attacked the counterfeiters, but they managed to escape through secret passages in the cliff and allegedly stashed their fake bills within the caverns.

Not all buried treasure stories are bogus. People did bury and hide valuables, especially at times in history when banks were seen as unreliable at best and predatory at worst. A story of discovering buried treasure comes from Lynn, Wisconsin, in a 1900 newspaper report: "While engaged in cutting down a maple tree that grew in his pasture, Andrew Olesen discovered a cavity near its base and on investigation found a wooden box about two feet square filled with loot. Among its contents were 150 silver dollars of American and Mexican vintage," dated 1846 to 1859, along with $200 in gold coins, gold and silver watch cases, candlesticks and silver cutlery. The newspaper noted that a skeleton had been found nearby the year before.

Another colorful treasure legend is the story of a "giant fur trader" nicknamed "Red Beard," who supposedly hid barrels of gold and silver in a hill near Crivitz.

Charles E. Brown assembled some of these stories into a 1945 booklet titled *Lost Treasure Tales: Some Wisconsin Lost Treasure Legends and Tales*. One of the stories from 1830 tells of a steamship named *The Idler* that was making its way up the Wisconsin River to Fort Winnebago, transporting a chest full of money. "When they reached the vicinity of the present river town of Lone Rock she struck a snag and tore a large hole in her bottom. She was sinking fast, and Captain Riggs ordered all ashore." The spot was hidden in what is now Dewey State Park in a location known as "Treasure Cave."

The money chest was brought to shore and buried at the base of the bluff, and stories vary as to whether or not it was ever recovered, leading to it being a popular spot for treasure hunters until a river highway was constructed there.

There is a legend about a buried supply of precious metal inside Silver Mound, near Alma Center in Jackson County, which was quarried by Native Americans for quartzite to make tools. It became a perennial spot targeted by miners, who believed silver to be buried there, first marked on a treasure map by French fur trader Pierre Charles LeSueur. His map, or copies of it, was handed down to other parties who tried their luck at striking silver throughout the 1800s. Native Americans say that there is silver in Silver Mound, but it is protected by a spirit that guards it from being found.

Here's a more contemporary treasure story from Milwaukee. In 1981, Byron Preiss authored a book, *The Secret: A Treasure Hunt*, which contains poems and illustrations with clues for readers on where buried treasures could be found across North America. Preiss buried twelve treasures—a ceramic "casque" in a plexiglass container that contains a key to a safety deposit box that holds a gem worth about $1,000. But Preiss hid these treasures a bit too well—only three out of twelve have been found. One was found the year after the book was published in Chicago's Grant Park, and the next one wasn't discovered until 2004 at Cleveland's Greek Cultural Garden; the last one to be discovered was found in Langone Park in Boston in 2019. Preiss died in a car accident in 2005, taking the locations of the remaining hidden treasures to his grave.

It is strongly believed that one of those concealed casques is in Milwaukee's Lake Park. An image in the book shows a juggler tossing a millstone, a walking stick and a key, clues that the city is "mill-walk-key." The poem instructs to "ascend the 92 steps," a number that matches up to a staircase in Lake Park. The juggler's face in the painting is also possibly an imitation of one of the stone lions found on one of the park's bridges.

Josh Gates, host of the Discovery Channel show *Expedition Unknown*, traveled to Milwaukee to try to find Lake Park's treasure for an episode that aired in 2018, but his attempt was cut short by a thunderstorm. He also failed to find one in St. Augustine, Florida, but in 2019, he joined a family who had pieced together clues and found Preiss's treasure hidden in Boston.

Who will find Preiss's Milwaukee treasure? Don't think you can show up with a shovel to dig up Lake Park until you find it—you need an entry permit issued by the Milwaukee County Department of Parks to excavate, and they are rarely granted. As of this writing, the secret remains hidden.

BIG FISH STORIES

One of Wisconsin's favorite outdoor pastimes is fishing, and many spots have developed mini-legends about "the one that got away." These big fish stories, shared with family and friends, become part of local lore. One of the most legendary was the capture of a world record–sized muskellunge (the Wisconsin State Fish) named "Chin Whiskered Charlie" in the Chippewa Flowage by Louie Spray in 1949, one of three record-breaking muskies he caught.

Left: Alton Von Camp shows off his friend Louie Spray's record-breaking fifty-nine-and-a-half-pound muskie. Hayward, Wisconsin, 1930. *Wisconsin Historical Society, image 96787.*

Above: Muskie-shaped exterior of the Fresh Water Hall of Fame and Museum. *Travelwisconsin.com.*

According to an account by Spray, he and a fishing partner took off from Herman's Landing on October 1, 1949, in the Chippewa Flowage and pursued the fish for nineteen days, finally catching him on October 20. From Spray's own account: "Everyone on the flowage knew about 'Chin Whiskered Charlie,' except no one would talk about it. They all wanted to go out there and get it themselves. I knew that big fellow was there. I'd been after him for several years myself and hooked him a number of times." This time, Spray hooked Charlie and engaged in a forty-minute-long battle to land the legendary fish, including shooting it twice in the head with a pistol, eventually pulling in the sixty-nine-pound, eleven-ounce muskie.

But the lore of the fish story didn't end when Spray landed the elusive muskie. There were allegations that Spray was a fraud and that locals exaggerated the length and weight of Chin Whiskered Charlie so Spray could win the title. World Record Muskie Alliance issued a challenge to the record, saying that Spray's catch was problematic, citing "local favoritism, outright cheating, and even unethical taxidermy."

To make the fish story even stranger, fisherman Spence Petros claimed that Chicago gangster Joey "The Doves" Aiuppa had told him that he was the one who caught the muskie Spray took credit for, selling the prizewinning fish for fifty dollars, not wanting to take credit because he was on the lam. Despite the allegations, Spray still holds the largest muskie record. Spray died in 1984, and unfortunately, his three record muskie mounts were destroyed in a fire.

The Fresh Water Fishing Hall of Fame and Museum in Hayward, Wisconsin, is shaped like a giant muskie and immortalizes Spray and other anglers who have had legendary encounters with fish by displaying their gear, honoring their achievements and sharing their life stories.

who worked in the timber industry as a land surveyor and later in life ran a resort near Rhinelander. He hung around lumberjack camps and, as you might recall from the last chapter, claims to be the originator of Paul Bunyan folklore. He was an early circulator of the tall tales, but taking his word on anything would be hard to do, as he was also a well-known practical joker.

Among his many pranks were fooling people at a resort he ran into believing he had a unique, rare breed of scented moss on the property (which was regular moss doused in perfume) and a fake muskie he had rigged up to leap out of the water to entice guests into taking fishing trips. He liked to enlist a friend to pinch people's legs on public transportation while he imitated a growling dog to fool them into thinking they had been bitten. To be in Shepard's vicinity was to be a practical joke victim in waiting.

Shepard's hoax with the longest-lasting impact began in 1893, when he claimed he had encountered a Hodag, a beast based on lumberjack folklore. A Hodag, lumberjacks believed, was the ghost of a disgruntled ox. In 1896, Shepard claimed he had captured the beast (by putting chloroform at the end

A posse reenacts the capture of the Hodag, 1899. Gene Shepard is standing far right, holding a pole. His son, Layton, is the Hodag's victim. *Rhinelander Historical Society*.

The Hodag statue outside the Rhinelander Visitor Center. *Rhinelander Area Chamber of Commerce.*

of a long pole and knocking the monster unconscious). Several other details about the life of the Hodag were embellished and reported by Shepard and others—that the Hodag preferred to dine on white bulldogs, for example, or that its young were delivered from a set of thirteen eggs.

He displayed his creature at the Oneida County Fair, but after scientists from the Smithsonian Institution announced that they were traveling to see the animal, Shepard admitted it was a hoax—he had created the creature out of wood, ox hide and bull horns. An assistant would move the sculpture with a stick and make growling noises in the dark tent.

A fire at his resort at Ballard Lake destroyed his original Hodag carving and Shepard died in 1923, but the Hodag lives on. Today, the Hodag is the symbol of Rhinelander sports teams, businesses and the annual Hodag Country Festival. A giant Hodag statue stands in front of the Rhinelander Chamber of Commerce, and a replica of the original carving can be found at the Lumberjack Museum. The strange creature is now one of the most notable aspects of Rhinelander, so perhaps Shepard has had the last laugh on the subject.

GOATMAN

There's an urban legend trope I like to classify as a "Lover's Lane Legend," which might have been invented to keep young hormonal teens away from dark, secluded make-out spots—but of course it had the opposite effect. A famous version of this urban legend is the tale of the "Hook Man." The story goes that a couple is making out in a car on the side of a quiet country lane when they hear a news bulletin on the radio that an inmate has escaped a nearby asylum. A scratching is heard on the car, and when the male gets out to investigate, he disappears. In most versions of the story, he's found murdered, usually hanging from a tree branch above the car. As the woman (or couple, if they survive) drive away to safety, the frightening discovery is later made that a hook is stuck in the car—a narrow escape from Hook Man. There are many variations on the Lover's Lane Legend that have all sorts of escaped maniacs, ghosts and ghouls.

A hideous half-man, half-goat creature with the obvious name "Goatman" is said to be the one that stalks at night on the desolate country lane Hogsback Road, located in Washington County near Holy Hill and the communities of Erin, Richfield and Hubertus.

The urban legend about Hogsback Road is that a newlywed couple was traveling the bumpy road in the 1870s. After a wagon wheel splintered on the harsh road, the husband said he would walk back to town to get help. That night, the woman, alone and frightened, heard footsteps and a bleating, animal-like snorting. There was a strong animal odor in the air. Peeking out of the wagon, she saw "a creature covered in coarse red hair standing on two legs like a man, but with the horned head and long muzzle of a goat," as the story goes, according to Wisconsin researcher and author J. Nathan Couch, who wrote a book exploring the subject titled *Goatman: Flesh or Folklore?*

With an ending similar to the Hook Man story, the poor abandoned wife leaves her wagon at dawn and follows hoofprints to a tree, where she finds her husband's mutilated remains hanging, a victim of Goatman. The urban legend says that motorists who dare to drive down Hogsback Road will find themselves stranded and a potential victim of Goatman, just like this couple from the 1870s.

The reason I chose to include Goatman here rather than in the urban legends chapter is that people have reported actual Goatman sightings. In his book, Couch explores similar legends and claims of people spotting the Goatman in different parts of the country walking among us. Another Goatman story comes from Louisville, Kentucky, where a Goatman creature

An artist's depiction of Goatman. *David Beyer Jr.*

known locally as the Pope Lick Monster, named after the Pope Lick Creek, lives under a railroad trestle that bridges over the creek. Legend trippers, apparently not aware that the train tracks are still in use, have died looking for the creature.

Couch's research led to an interesting story and a possible seed of some of the urban myths. Couch uncovered a famous vagabond named Ches McCartney, aka the "Goat Man," who traveled around in a wagon pulled by a team of goats. His travels brought him to Washington County in the summer of 1949. McCartney was often arrested on trumped-up charges and treated cruelly by media and passersby because of his eccentric lifestyle and team of goats, and time possibly changed his story and made him a satyr.

The Beast of Bray Road

One of the most classic monsters of mythology is the werewolf. But could something like that actually be real? In the early 1990s, Elkhorn, Wisconsin, grabbed headlines around the world with reports that residents had been spotting a werewolf-like creature lurking around country lanes. The story has made the "Beast of Bray Road" one of Wisconsin's most famous monster stories.

The sign for Bray Road. *Lacy Landre*.

The first reporter to dig into the story was Linda S. Godfrey, who interviewed witnesses and then stopped by an animal control center where a worker showed her a folder with reports that he had labeled "Werewolf." Something strange was going on in Elkhorn. The creature got its moniker because the majority of the sightings were near Bray Road, a small, sparsely populated country lane surrounded by farmland. It's here the monster was spotted running across the lane, through cornfields, gnawing on roadkill on the side of the road and, in one case, attacking a car.

Soon, news vans and shows like *Inside Edition* were rolling into Elkhorn, the local bakery was selling Beast of Bray Road cookies, bars were offering "Silver Bullet Specials" and Bray Road was well trafficked by lookie-loos cruising around hoping to have a Beast sighting of their own. Godfrey eventually packaged the case study into a book titled *The Beast of Bray Road: Tailing Wisconsin's Werewolf.*

Since then, Godfrey has become the world's leading expert on "Manwolves," as she calls them (as they haven't been reported to transform like werewolves do), and received more reports not just from other locations in Wisconsin (and Michigan, where they're more commonly known as "Dogmen") but from around the country and the world. Godfrey has written several books on the Manwolves topic, as well as monster sightings and other strange

Artist's depiction of the Beast of Bray Road. *David Beyer Jr.*

phenomena, including books like *Real Wolfmen: True Encounters in Modern America* and *American Monsters: A History of Monster Lore, Legends, and Sightings in America.* The Beast is still occasionally spotted on occasion in the Elkhorn area and other locations. In one case near Holy Hill, a contractor with the DNR was collecting roadkill and claimed that he witnessed a Manwolf poaching a dead deer from the back of his truck.

The Beast remains a favorite case study of cryptozoology. In 2017, a documentary titled *The Bray Road Beast* was released by Seth Breedlove as part of his Small Town Monsters documentary series, with several local interviews and footage being shot in Elkhorn.

BIGFOOT

The most legendary unknown entity of North America is Sasquatch, also known as Bigfoot and by a variety of regional nicknames. This creature, whatever it might be, has been spotted from the Pacific Northwest, where it first became well known, to the desert and mountain states and the forests of the East Coast. In fact, every state in the union except Hawaii has had at least one Bigfoot sighting. The woods of the Midwest, including Wisconsin, are especially known as hot spots for sightings.

In particular, most Bigfoot sightings come from within the massive Kettle Moraine State Forest, which spreads for hundreds of miles and is divided into a northern unit and a southern unit. Besides attracting hikers

Bigfoot was here? *Jay Bachochin/WPI Hunts the Truth.*

and others seeking to enjoy the outdoors, Kettle Moraine is a destination for Bigfooters.

The nation's largest Bigfoot research group, the Bigfoot Field Researchers Organization (BFRO), has a few local representatives, Jen and Larry Dopke, who have led expeditions into the Kettle Moraine. An episode of the reality show *Finding Bigfoot* featured the Dopkes joining their BFRO teammates on an investigation in northern Wisconsin in an episode titled "Brews, Brats, and Bigfoot."

Jay Bachochin runs his organization called Wisconsin Paranormal Investigators (WPI) Hunts the Truth and has also spent time investigating the Kettle Moraine. Bachochin shared evidence that he believes are from Bigfoot encounters on his website (wpihuntsthetruth.com). He's also produced a documentary titled *Finding Jay*, which presents his research, including photos of footprints said to belong to the Wisconsin Sasquatch.

In East Troy, the local Bigfoot is known as "Eddy" (rhymes with "Yeti"), according to Linda S. Godfrey's book *Wisconsin Monsters*. "A woman who grew up in East Troy told me that cruising around the area between East Troy and Palmyra to look for the Eddy was a standard dating ritual," Godfrey wrote.

Others in the Jefferson/Walworth County area report a hairy creature called the Bluff Monster that lurks by Bluff Road, which runs through the Kettle Moraine near Palmyra. More Bigfoot sightings have occurred all over the state, including Delavan, Fort Atkinson and in Walworth County on the Highway DD–Honey Creek Bridge.

HELLHOUNDS

Hellhounds exist in the lore of many locations and are depicted as large, black-furred dogs with glowing red eyes of hellfire that do the bidding of Satan himself. Although sometimes they are spotted, they are often said to be invisible, with their hideous snarling as the only warning you have that you are being stalked by such a creature.

Caryville, located in Dunn County, is rich with ghostlore, including stories of hauntings at the Caryville Church and a historic schoolhouse. Caryville Road is said to be home to a ghost of a drunken prom queen who swerved and crashed on a bridge where phantom cars can be spotted. It's also said that on stormy nights at midnight, a pack of hellhounds runs down Caryville Road.

Near Caryville, on the banks of the Chippewa River, there is a boat landing and cemetery. The island in the river across from the boat landing is former home to a settlement called Meridean, which was abandoned due to a dwindling lumber industry and frequent flooding, leaving the community a ghost town. Local lore says the island was supposedly the former home to a sanatorium guarded by the hellhounds.

The boat landing location is a hangout spot for partying teens, who are known to dare one another to park near the landing at the bottom of the hill near the cemetery and turn off their headlights, an act said to bring the hellhounds out. The island is reportedly named after Mary Dean, a woman who either committed suicide or accidentally drowned in the river, which her siren-like ghost still haunts, trying to lure others to a watery grave. The hellhounds are perhaps her paranormal accomplices.

A 2015 episode of *Monsters and Mysteries in America* featured the Caryville Hellhound story, bringing it further notoriety. In the show, a couple shares an encounter from 2005. They said they were enjoying a picnic by the infamous boat landing. When the sun went down, a fog rolled in, and an invisible force came stomping and growling toward them, chasing them away.

LAKE MONSTERS

The most famous lake monster in the world is the Loch Ness Monster, but unknown creatures have been spotted in bodies of water all over, and Wisconsin is no exception. America's Dairyland has a higher number of sightings than most states due to its plethora of lakes and rivers.

In his book *Lake Monsters of Wisconsin*, researcher and chronicler of the weird Chad Lewis lists historic accounts of monsters dwelling in a wide range of Wisconsin bodies of water, including the Mississippi and Rock Rivers and lakes from the Great (Michigan and Superior) variety to the small, like Lake Koshkonong, which is only seven feet at its deepest.

The majority of Wisconsin lake monster sightings occurred from the late 1800s to about 1920, dwindling considerably after that. Many of the classic lake monster reports were collected by Wisconsin folklore historian Charles E. Brown and published in his monograph *Sea Serpents: Wisconsin Occurrences of These Weird Water Monsters in the Four lakes, Rock, Red Cedar, Koshkonong, Geneva, Elkhart, Michigan, and Other Lakes*, published by the Wisconsin Folklore Society in 1942. Here's a rundown of the most well-known Wisconsin lake monster sightings.

LAKE WINNEBAGO MONSTER: Stories of a monster in Lake Winnebago, which is 215 square miles of water, date back to Ho-Chunk native lore that says a beast dwells in the lake that ambushes and eats moose, elk and deer, so the waters were treated carefully. There were reported sightings of a creature in 1887–89 and then again in 1891.

ROCKY: Reported sightings of "Rocky," or the "Rock Lake Terror," in Jefferson County's Rock Lake include encounters with both fishermen and boaters. The most famous of these stories came from 1882, when two men named Ed McKenzie and D.W. Seybert were racing rowboats across the lake. McKenzie's vessel was approached by the lake monster, which he later described as being as big as his boat. The monster's head lifted about three feet out of the water, and it opened its jaws before diving back in. McKenzie prepared to attack the beast by hitting it with his oar. Witnesses on shore cruised out with a gun to help in the battle, but the creature had taken off by the time they arrived. Ed was so scared his face lost color and his teeth were chattering, according to reports. The creature left a "sickening odor" behind.

In another encounter, a man named Fred Seaver reported that the sea serpent "seized his trolling hook and pulled his boat along over half a mile at a rushing speed before he let go," Charles E. Brown recorded. The last reported sighting of the creature was in 1943.

JENNY: Lake Geneva's Jenny, described as being a thirty-to-sixty-five-foot serpent or dinosaur-like creature, is famous for capsizing boats. There is supposedly local Potawatomi lore of a monster dwelling in the lake, which the tribe assigned blame for tipping canoes and persons who mysteriously went missing. There used to be an effigy mound nearby of a giant lizard or serpent before settlers developed the area. In the 1890s, there were reports of capsized or overturned boats, and on July 22, 1892, a man and two boys were allegedly chased from the lake by a monster that bellowed at them, as reported by the *Chicago Tribune*. On August 12, 1899, the *Wisconsin State Journal* reported a thirty-foot monster being spotted in the lake. In 1902, however, the *Lake Geneva Herald* speculated that Jenny had been a fabrication made up by Chicago journalists to sell newspapers.

BOZHO: Named after the native trickster spirit Winnebozho, this lake monster was spotted in Madison on Lake Mendota from the 1860s to the 1890s by people fishing and boating. In 1883, Madison fisherman Billy Dunn said that he encountered an enormous serpent, green with white spots, that hissed, stuck out its forked tongue and bit his oar. Billy's response was beating the creature with a paddle until it retreated to the depths of the lake.

In 1892, there were several sightings of Bozho and a few organized hunts to try to find the creature, which successfully evaded capture. Stories of people having face-to-face encounters with Bozho continued over the next decade, including a wave of strange meetings in 1917. The most unusual was an incident with a young woman and man bathing at the end of a fraternity house pier when the woman reportedly felt something tickling her feet. She sat up to see "the head and neck of a huge snake, or dragon" had been licking her feet with a "friendly, humorous look in its big eyes." Bozho continued to cause mischief by reportedly overturning canoes, chasing sailboats and frightening swimmers until sightings dwindled by the 1940s, although the legend is still shared in Madison.

PEPIE: Lake Pepin borders Wisconsin and Minnesota, and a creature known as Pepie has been spotted from both sides of the lake, including a wave of 1875 appearances. One description of the animal noted that it was "between the size of an elephant and a rhinoceros, which moves through the water with great rapidity." Unlike many of the lake monsters on this list, there were contemporary sightings in the 1970s and even as recent as 2008 and 2010.

Lake City, Minnesota, is the unofficial Pepie headquarters, where a shop called Treats & Treasures is an "Official Pepie Watch Station" where people can buy Pepie merchandise and stop in to find out about sightings. Lake City businessman Larry Nielson runs a Pepie website and offers a $50,000 reward for anyone who captures proof of its existence. There was a Pepie Fest (2015), and you can board a Pepie Expedition and Cruise.

LAKE KOSHKONONG MONSTER: Native lore says that the lake was home to a giant monster and that entering or trying to cross it in canoe would lead to death. In November 1887, two duck hunters from Milwaukee saw a thirty-foot serpent cruising through the lake, which they pursued in an attempt to capture, but it disappeared into thin air. Later, a farmer on the west side of the lake claimed that a monster had stolen some of his pigs. The trail of the Lake Koshkonong Monster sightings runs dry after the 1887 encounter, although a "Wake the Monster" charity motorcycle ice race is held on the frozen lake in winter to celebrate the legendary lake monster.

DEVIL'S LAKE MONSTERS: The monster lore of Devil's Lake comes from a variety of different places. There are native legends of the giant

The mysterious Devil's Lake. *Anna Rodriguez*.

Thunderbirds (*wakhakeera*) battling water monsters (*wakunja*) for days to form the lake. Another tells of a seven-headed dragon that lived in the lake and required annual sacrifice of a maiden until a tribe led by a young brave named River-Child defeated him. Other stories include a giant octopus and/or plesiosaur type of creature.

In the 1970s, Devil's Lake was thought to be a Cthulhu Power Zone, where black magick rituals were carried out in the hopes of summoning monsters referred to as the "Deep Ones." Cthulhu and the Deep Ones were fictitious characters created in the works of horror writer H.P. Lovecraft. The attempts are recalled in occultist Kenneth Grant's 1975 book *Cults of the Shadow*.

RED CEDAR LAKE MONSTER: In 1890, the *Oshkosh Daily Northwestern* reported that a local farmer saw a "reptile forty feet long" carry off one of his hogs. On September 5, 1891, the *Janesville Gazette* noted that "the cedar lake sea serpent is again making trouble," but after sharing a story, the paper added that there were "some doubts are expressed as to the truthfulness of this report, as the man who claims to have been an eyewitness of this occurrence is not noted for his truth and voracity."

MOTHMAN AND MINERAL POINT VAMPIRE

In 2016, a new terror was flapping in the Midwest. It was an entity soon dubbed the "Lake Michigan Mothman."

The original Mothman sightings are part of the lore of the Point Pleasant, West Virginia area. From 1966 to 1967, Point Pleasant residents reported seeing an odd gray humanoid with glowing red eyes and wings that was terrorizing the town by swooping down at cars and appearing in people's yards.

In 2016, reports of a similar Mothman-type creature began to file in from the Chicago area. A woman in Wauconda, Illinois, reported seeing a hairy black figure with leathery wings hunched over in the street while she was taking out her garbage in April 2016. When it approached her, she quickly retreated into her house, and when she looked again, it was gone. Over the next three years, similar reports of supernatural activity have come in from Illinois, Indiana, Michigan and Wisconsin.

Several midwestern researchers have investigated these stories, including Tobias and Emily Wayland of the Singular Fortean Society, who have a definitive timeline of these types of sightings posted on their website. They have produced a book written by Tobias titled *The Lake Michigan Mothman: High Strangeness in the Midwest.* They believe that some of the sightings are probably misidentification of known animals, but some of the encounters could be paranormal. Tobias reported:

> So far, six reported "Mothman" sightings that took place in Wisconsin have been added to our timeline of events: A woman and her family reported seeing a "man with bat-like features" flying near their vehicle while [they were] driving on a desolate stretch of Highway 59 near Road X in southern Wisconsin in mid-July, 2006; A woman reported seeing a "man-like" being with "pterodactyl-like" wings gliding across a highway outside of Whitewater in 2016; A man reported an encounter with a humanoid "bat-dragon" near Mukwonago in mid-April, 2017; A couple in Milwaukee were reportedly terrified by a bat-like flying humanoid with "large glowing red eyes" on April 13, 2018; A woman driving to work near Darien said she almost struck a "flying witch" with her car on February 25, 2019; and ghost hunter Kane Adams collided with a "miniature Mothman"—which reportedly survived the encounter—while driving his semi-truck near Wittenberg on April 12, 2019.

Of these, Tobias says the 2017 Mukwonago sighting is the most frightening. The witness had returned to his parents' home late one evening and was talking on his phone around 10:45 p.m.:

> As he was speaking, he glanced up into the damp night and only a few feet beyond the hood of his vehicle, lit by the ambient light of a nearby light post, he saw what he described as a "seven-foot bat/reptile of some sort." The being had "large black eyeballs…[and] skin or scales of some kind," and "huge wings…wrapped around its body, exactly as a bat wraps its wings around its body while sleeping upside-down."

About twelve seconds later, the being disappeared in a blur in the headlights. The Waylands later met and interviewed the witness. "The fear this man felt was very real and very apparent as he recounted events—even in broad daylight," Tobias said.

On April 13, 2018, the creature was reportedly spotted again, this time in Milwaukee, where a couple says they were in a dark parking lot and saw the Mothman, which they estimated to be seven feet tall with glowing red eyes. They heard screeching and flapping of wings as they sped out of the parking lot and saw the creature fly away.

A case that predates these Mothman sightings is a story from La Crosse on September 26, 2006. A man and his son were driving on Briggs Road and spotted what was dubbed the "La Crosse Man Bat," with the witnesses describing a humanoid creature with a ten-foot wingspan. The creature proceeded to dive-bomb the vehicle, swooping over the windshield and disappearing into the night sky.

An illustration based on sightings of the Lake Michigan Mothman. *Emily Wayland/Singular Fortean Society.*

THE STRANGEST LEGACY OF Mineral Point, located in southwest Wisconsin, is a recurring episode of sightings of what has come to be known as the Mineral Point Vampire.

The story starts in 1981 at Graceland Cemetery. Police were called to investigate what people reported as a vampire wandering around the tombstones. Officer John Pepper responded and saw the alleged night stalker. He gave pursuit, but the vampire escaped by leaping over a six-foot wall.

The Mineral Point Vampire (or perhaps a relative of his) appears to have returned in 2004, when it was reported that he was jumping out of trees and attacking residents of an apartment near Graceland Cemetery, with a similar description of the vampire in the 1981 case. Police were called and gave chase, but, the story goes, the vampire escaped again by leaping over a wall. A third encounter was reported in 2008 when a couple on a fishing trip saw the vampire, who had snuck up on them. The couple reported that they ran to their car and made a quick getaway.

Out-of-Place Animals

Occasionally, we hear reports of an animal on the loose that doesn't fit in with Wisconsin's native fauna. The circuses are no longer headquartered here, but Wisconsin has no state laws on the books regulating ownership of exotic animals as pets, at least as of this writing. As you'll soon read, some of these sightings have led to a call to reexamine these lax animal regulations.

Mystery Kangaroos: Unless you're at a zoo, spotting a kangaroo hopping along in Wisconsin is sure to make you do a double-take. There was quite a commotion on April 5, 1978, when a roo was spotted in morning rush hour traffic in Waukesha. A school bus driver reported seeing two kangaroos hopping across Highway A and Moreland Boulevard. A dozen more reports came from Waukesha, as well as nearby locations in Brookfield and Pewaukee. A Waukesha tavern organized a kangaroo hunt that came up empty-handed. A man named Richard Schmitt claimed that the sightings were a hoax and that he, with the help of his brother and a friend, had created a kangaroo cutout out of plywood that had fooled everyone.

Another kangaroo encounter happened in early January 2005 when a kangaroo was discovered in Iowa County, near Dodgeville, in a snowstorm. This time, though, the roo was tracked down, corralled into a barn, shot with a tranquilizer dart and captured, although where he came from is still unknown. A local author named Jean Rennebohm wrote a children's book titled *The Mystery Kangaroo—It's Absolutely True* about the animal, calling him Boomer. Boomer lived out the rest of his days at the Henry Vilas Zoo. The kangaroo was somewhat old when found and died at the zoo in 2008, but he lives on in the form of a statue commemorating the mystery animal.

Milwaukee Lion: The year 2015 featured what I dubbed the "Summer of the Lion," in which people began reporting a string of lion sightings, complete with a fuzzy video from its first appearance on July 20. Police Chief Edward Flynn admitted that it "certainly seemed to be a lion-ish creature" in response to the strange reports. Milwaukee finally had a Bigfoot-level legend. Lion fever hit Milwaukee as Mayor Barrett cracked feline jokes and social media blew up with photoshopped lions at famous Milwaukee landmarks. Major national news outlets picked up the story. Within a few days, more than two dozen lion sightings had been phoned in. The climax of the Milwaukee Lion story was July 27, when police believed they had the lion surrounded. They tried to lure it out with a tantalizing trap of summer sausage, turkey and Chicken McNuggets. The wily lion slipped away—most likely scared off by the large, noisy crowd of media and lion gawkers—and disappeared into the ether. Lion sightings dried up by early August, and the Milwaukee Lion was forgotten.

Milwaukee Lion believers felt vindicated in February 2018, when a clear home security video revealed that a home in nearby Brookfield did have a visit by a large mountain lion; it peeked into their window, leaving paw prints behind. Where the Milwaukee Lion roams now is still a mystery.

PART IV

GHOSTLORE

In the classic book *Wisconsin Lore*, authors L.G. Sorden and Robert E. Gard wrote, "Wisconsin may have more ghosts per square mile than any other state." I think they were probably right—almost every Wisconsin town has a story to share. Ghosts haunt hotels, theaters, breweries and people's homes. Nearly every building with a history seems to have left a spirit behind.

It's impossible to record all of Wisconsin's ghostlore here, so I chose to share some of our state's most famous apparitions. These range from tales dating back to before Wisconsin became a state to contemporary stories. I gave some particular preference to stories that have a distinctly Wisconsin twist to them. Hearing ghost stories is a great cultural experience, as these tales often teach us about interesting chapters of Wisconsin history.

MILWAUKEE: PFISTER HOTEL

Milwaukee has so many allegedly haunted locations that the city could be rebranded as "Ghost City" instead of "Brew City." Milwaukee ghostlorist Allison Jornlin has meticulously tracked supernatural experiences around the city, and the reports keep her and local groups like Paranormal Investigators of Milwaukee and Brew City Paranormal busy on expeditions to these allegedly haunted locations. You'll find stories of spirits that haunt the Brumder Mansion, the Pabst Mansion, the Miller Caves, Milwaukee Public Museum and many other locations.

The city's most well-known ghostlore, though, comes from the beautiful and historic Pfister Hotel, which opened in 1893. The hotel's namesake, Charles Pfister, was a Renaissance man, a partner in the Pfister and Vogel tannery, a bank financier and newspaper publisher, a political backer and a philanthropist who donated large sums of his money to art and charity groups. His longest-lasting achievement is the Pfister Hotel, located in the heart of downtown Milwaukee. Pfister's father, Guido Pfister, had a vision of building the most magnificent hotel in the city, and Pfister fulfilled this vision with a project that had a price tag of more than $1 million (more than $27 million in today's money). The hotel was outfitted with all the latest amenities, including features that at the time were cutting-edge, like fireproofing, electricity and temperature control by thermostat. From the time it was built, it's been a world-class hotel and continues to draw celebrities and famous political guests from around the world.

Allison Jornlin's research found that after Charles Pfister's death in 1927, the staff at the hotel reported seeing his ghost (a portrait in the hotel lobby helps identify him) and have expressed mostly positive experiences—they've seen Pfister watching over staff from the second floor of the lobby, standing in the elevator or walking his ghost dog through the hall, giving them the impression that he is benignly making sure his hotel is running smoothly.

The reputation of these ghost stories began to change in the early 2000s, when the hotel became just as notorious among Major League Baseball players as it was with paranormal investigators. One of my prized possessions is an album of baseball cards I've collected featuring players who have had supernatural experiences at the Pfister. The collection has twenty-five players…so far.

Members of the Reds, Marlins and Phillies, among others, have claimed to have had frightening experiences, including hearing ghostly footsteps, scratching on the walls, witnessing electronic devices turning off and on by themselves and seeing full-bodied apparitions.

Adrian Beltre, who played with the Dodgers during his experience, was one of the first baseball players to be brave enough to share his otherworldly encounter in 2001. He said that after hearing strange knocking and his TV and air conditioner turning on and off by themselves in his hotel room, he chose to sleep that night with his baseball bat by his side.

In 2008, Carlos Gomez of the Minnesota Twins was frightened after he heard a disembodied whisper while he was in the shower. When he got out

The Pfister Hotel. *Rita Lange.*

to investigate, he saw his iPod flick on and off as it moved across a table by itself. He decided to grab his clothes and finished getting dressed in the lobby. In another story, Bryce Harper of the Nationals reported that when he returned to his room, he discovered that his clothes had been tossed around the room.

Colby "Cobra" Lewis hit a home run and takes the title for the most frightening experience at the Pfister with his story. In 2010, the Texas Ranger claimed to have seen a "skeletal apparition" in his room around 1:30 a.m. Four or five other fellow Rangers also reported having weird experiences that night. Lewis was so frightened that he consulted the team's chaplain and skipped an ESPN radio interview the next day. His teammate C.J. Wilson filled in on the show and reported his own encounter—ghostly scratching on his walls and a lamp that turned on and off by itself.

The stories have continued for the last twenty years. Recent accounts include Ji-Man Choi, who claimed that he felt a spirit sharing his bed with him at the Pfister in 2016 when he was in town for a game playing with the Los Angeles Angels. In June 2018, St. Louis Cardinals teammates Carlos Martinez and outfielder Marcell Ozuna both spotted what they described as a ghostly torso that appeared in the air, which prompted them to retreat to team member Francisco Peña's room for safety, where a frightened Martinez reported on the situation via an Instagram live video: "We are all here. We are in Peñita's room. We are all stuck here. We are going to sleep here on the floor…if the ghost shows again, we are all going to fight together," Martinez reported in Spanish.

Why the ghosts seem to target baseball players (although actor Joey Lawrence also reported an eerie encounter at the hotel on the show *Celebrity Ghost Story*) is unknown. Perhaps this is a ghostly assist from Charles Pfister, trying to give the Milwaukee Brewers a spook-out advantage? The baseball stories have led to some urban legends with no historical basis about the hotel, such as a suicide at the hotel when a man discovered his wife was having an affair with a baseball player or other similar dramatic stories.

MILWAUKEE: THE RAVE/EAGLE'S BALLROOM

The historic Eagles Club building, built in 1927, reflects a more prosperous time for the neighborhood in which it is located, which in years past was full of mansions that belonged to the beer barons and other prominent Milwaukeeans (the nearby historic Brumder and Pabst Mansions are both also said to be haunted). The Eagles Club was run by the Fraternal Order of Eagles and was a recreation center that included a gymnasium, bowling alley, basketball court, boxing ring, lounges, barbershop, cafeteria, pool hall and even a radio station, among other amenities.

The crown jewel was the ballroom, one of the largest of its kind when it was built, with big band, theater and other performances entertaining a room with a capacity of thousands. In 1959, it cost $1.50 to see the first date of the Winter Party tour at the ballroom with Buddy Holly, the Big Bopper and Ritchie Valens, just ten days before the three musicians died in a plane crash in Iowa.

By the 1980s, the building had fallen into disrepair and was put up for sale. It was remodeled in the 1990s and rebranded The Rave, with many of the spaces turned into bars and various-sized venue spaces spread throughout the building. The ballroom space is still used for concerts of all genres today, including lots of rock, metal, hip hop and country shows.

Rumors of ghostly activity have long been associated with the building. The most famous ghost story involves the Eagles Club's vacant swimming pool, which still exists but has sat empty and closed off to the public for decades. Allegedly a little girl drowned there and haunts the pool area, and her ghostly laughter can be heard echoing in the room. Like a lot of ghost stories, there's an actual story to this legend—in 1927, a fifteen-year-old boy named Francis Wren died there. Carl Swanson of the website Milwaukee Notebook wrote an article revealing that the death was mysterious—the autopsy determined that drowning was the cause of death, but as Swanson reported, "No one has ever explained how an athletic young man, known to be an expert swimmer and diver, could have drowned, unnoticed, in a pool full of people." Despite urban legend stories, the pool was not closed off because of the drowning, but rather was emptied when the club was shut down.

Elsewhere in the building, a former employee named "Jack" is apparently still hanging around and haunting those who enter the boiler room, angrily chastising people who trespass on his turf. At some point, a homeless shelter was housed in the basement of The Rave while the building was sitting in disrepair, and a mean shelter manager is said to be one of the spirits remaining in the building. Urban legend also says the souls of Buddy Holly and sometimes his tour mates Ritchie Valens and the Big Bopper are still hanging around, their shadowy figures spotted in the ballroom, even though they died in Iowa.

The Rave/Eagles Club. *Rita Lange.*

Both employees and musicians performing at the club have reported eerie encounters, including seeing shadowy figures in the ballroom before and after shows, as well as lights and showers turning on and off by themselves. Some musicians have even labeled it as one of the "most haunted venues in America."

In 2017, indie record label Tooth & Nail Records of Seattle featured a special episode of its podcast *Labeled* called "The Rave in Milwaukee Is the Scariest Club in America," featuring bands on its label reporting their creepy experiences at the venue. The podcast also helped reveal some of the myths associated with The Rave/Eagles Club due to its proximity to the site of the former apartment building of Milwaukee serial killer Jeffrey Dahmer, where he murdered, dismembered and sometimes cannibalized his seventeen victims.

Musicians claimed that Dahmer lived across the street from the Eagles Club. He did live close but was actually about three and a half blocks away on Twenty-Fifth Street, in an apartment building that was demolished shortly after his conviction in 1992. The site is now an abandoned lot. Some of the confusion might be because Dahmer did kill one person when he stayed in a room in the Ambassador Hotel, which is close to The Rave. It was there that his first Milwaukee victim was killed in 1987, and he smuggled the body out of the hotel in a suitcase. Dahmer was living with his grandmother in West Allis at the time.

The claim that Dahmer frequented the Eagles Club gymnasium and pool looking for victims is also not true. Those facilities had shut down by the time he moved to Milwaukee, and he stalked many of his victims around the Walker's Point neighborhood bars and bus stops.

Baraboo: Highway 12 Phantom Hitchhiker

The Phantom Hitchhiker is an urban legend you'll find repeated throughout the country. These ghostly lost souls include brides in wedding dresses, runaways and soldiers, the latter of which seems to be the case on Highway 12, where a ghostly hitchhiker has been spotted at night along the highway stretching from Baraboo to the Wisconsin Dells.

The man people report seeing on the side of the road is dressed in an old green army jacket and jeans, sometimes described as having a beard and long hair. He is said to look as though he stepped out of the 1960s, possibly a Vietnam veteran. People supposedly see him trying to hitch a ride, usually at night, and then inexplicably see him again miles down the road as if he's projected himself ahead of them. Those brave enough to stop to give him a ride find that the phantom has disappeared by the time they pull over.

Paranormal researchers have tried to track down historical information about a death that might fit this ghost profile, to no avail.

PESHTIGO: PESHTIGO FIRE MUSEUM

The Great Chicago Fire of October 8, 1871, is a famous American tragedy that, because it happened in a major city, overshadows the more massive disaster approximately 250 miles north of it on the same day. The Great Peshtigo Fire also started on October 8, along with fires in Holland and Port Huron, both in Michigan. Extreme drought, along with strong winds and the common practice of slash-and-burn farming, left the Midwest vulnerable to fire. The Peshtigo fire killed between 1,500 and 2,500 people, more than four times the number of Chicago fatalities. The fire also set ablaze more than 1 million acres of forest, spreading over several counties in the vicinity of Peshtigo.

The heat created wind, which transformed the fire into what was described as a "tornado of flames," resulting in many people being stricken with hypothermia after they jumped in the Peshtigo River to try to escape the flames. People burned to death, were hit by fireballs or asphyxiated in the smoke-filled air. Peshtigo was completely wiped out—almost every building burned to the ground. Across Green Bay on the Door County peninsula, a second fire erupted on the same day. Many believe that the blast blew across the bay, but it was a separate fire.

A church in Champion, Wisconsin (just outside of Green Bay), now called the National Shrine of Our Lady of Good Help, had a Belgian immigrant parishioner named Adele Brise who reported having visions of Mary (which is called a Marian apparition) surrounded by bright light, clothed in white, with a crown of stars, on three separate occasions in 1859. As the fire broke out twelve years later, Brise led a group to pray to Mary for protection. The flames destroyed the surrounding lands, the story goes, but spared the chapel and its grounds. In 2010, the Catholic Church recognized Brise's visions as the first and only official Marian apparition sighting in the United States. The chapel was also approved as a diocesan shrine (a sacred place).

The Peshtigo Fire Museum. *Peshtigo Historical Society.*

Paranormal researchers have investigated the Peshtigo Fire Museum, housed in a former church and filled with artifacts from the fire. People have seen and smelled phantom flames and have heard voices inside the museum. The Peshtigo Fire Cemetery, which features a mass grave of fire victims, is also said to be haunted, with shadowy figures that have been spotted in the graveyard and on the road in front of it, as well as certain spots along the river where people died as they attempted to escape. It's also said that a ghost called the Lady in White hangs out in a park in Peshtigo on South Ellis Avenue.

LAND O' LAKES: SUMMERWIND

Former Hoover administration secretary of commerce Robert Patterson Lamont built along West Bay Lake in northeast Wisconsin the twenty-six-room Lamont Mansion (later renamed and now commonly known as Summerwind) as a summer home for his family in 1916. Ghost stories date back to this period, with the most famous one involving the phantom intruder that Lamont spotted in his basement doorway and at which he fired a few rounds.

After Lamont's death, the mansion was sold a few times until the early 1970s, when the Hinshaw family—Arnold, Ginger and their six children—moved into it. The ghost stories about the Hinshaw family's brief time in the house are legendary. A sinister entity or entities, the story goes, slowly drove the family insane.

The Hinshaws reportedly first began to see strange shapes and shadows in the hallways and hear mumbling voices in the dark. They found that doors and windows opened and shut by themselves and spotted an apparition of a woman floating in the air near the dining room.

Supposedly, the family found a corpse hidden behind a shoe drawer in the wall of a closet, but like a lot of stories spun about Summerwind, it's hard to be sure what parts of the tale might have a grain of truth and what was fabricated.

It is said that poor Arnold went insane from all this ghostly activity, staying up late at night to play loud, frenzied, nonsensical music on the family's Hammond organ, frightening his wife and kids, who huddled together in a bedroom. He claimed that a demon commanded him to play the organ.

Summerwind Mansion, 1985. *Todd Roll.*

Ginger reportedly attempted suicide, and Arnold was sent to a mental institute, while Ginger and the kids moved in with her parents in Granton, Wisconsin, where Ginger remarried.

Ginger's father, Raymond Bober, bought Summerwind, intending to turn it into a restaurant and inn, apparently not clued in by Ginger of the horrific haunting activity. Bober claimed to have had communication with the spirit haunting Summerwind, which he said he was named Jonathan Carver, a British explorer. Carver told Bober (through dreams, trances and a Ouija board) that he had a deed from the Sioux natives that entitled him to a third of Wisconsin and that the deed was hidden in the foundation of Summerwind. The ghost of Carver wanted Bober's help finding the hidden paper. Bober wove the story in a book he authored under the pen name Wolfgang von Bober titled *The Carver Effect*, published in 1979.

By 1988, the mansion was in a dilapidated state of disrepair. It was destroyed after lightning struck, and the abandoned house caught on fire; most of the building was destroyed except the foundation and stone chimneys. Summerwind and its unique history have since been a favorite story among ghostlorists and paranormal investigators. Attempts have been made by organizations to restore the mansion based on its original blueprints but have thus far failed.

Horicon: The Tallman House

Located on a quiet dead-end road called Larabee Street in the small town of Horicon, Debbie and Allen Tallman and their children found fifteen minutes of fame with a tale that was reminiscent of other haunting "based on a true story" tales like *The Amityville Horror* (a 1977 book that became a movie in 1979). After nine terror-filled months, the Tallman family said they fled their plain-looking, one-floor townhouse in 1988 after a series of terrifying events, including sightings of apparitions and phantom fires.

The evil spirit in the house, a poltergeist entity (a supernatural force that throws objects and makes noise), was said to be attached to a second-hand bunk bed the family had bought. Upon adding the piece of furniture to their home, strange occurrences began to happen at the Tallman house—a radio switched stations randomly, doors slammed shut by themselves, a chair and suitcase moved across the floor and disembodied voices were heard coming from empty rooms. A pastor claimed that the Tallmans' case was a demonic presence in the house and blessed it, but the paranormal activity didn't stop.

In fact, as the website Cult of Weird reported, things got more intense. The family witnessed "frightening visions of a haggard old woman" in the children's bedroom. Allen, the father, heard a voice in the garage beckoning him to "come here," and when he went to look, he discovered a phantom fire in the garage and a pair of red glowing eyes staring at him in the window. On another occasion, a foggy phantom mist materialized and turned into flame with green eyes that said, "You're dead" to Allen before disappearing.

All of this "pushed the family to the fringes of their sanity until, finally, they packed some bags and escaped the nightmare on the night of January 11 (1988)," as Cult of Weird noted. Gossip quickly spread in the community of Horicon.

"By the end of the week, the town was whispering about bleeding walls, [and] a hole to hell in the basement," the site reported, along with this rich Wisconsin supernatural claim: a "ghost-powered snowblower cleaned the driveway by itself." The media picked up the story, and soon Larabee Street was overrun by hordes of people, some of them intoxicated, who wanted to get a glimpse of the ghost. They walked through yards, climbed fences, peeked in windows and tried to break into the abandoned Tallman house. Arrests were made for drunk driving and other offenses, and the scene was so bad that the street was temporarily barricaded.

The Tallmans sold the house after moving out, and the story gained further attention when a segment about the haunting was included in an episode of *Unsolved Mysteries* on October 26, 1988, which featured clips shot inside the house, with the new owner's permission. "I'd wake up in the night crying, and I'd ask Allen if I was going to have nightmares like this all my life. I would dream that my kids were dying, that Allen was dying, that my father was dying," a disturbed Debbie Tallman said in the episode.

The Tallman family later reported that they had buried the troublesome bunk bed at an undisclosed private landfill. Some accused the Tallman family of seeking a story deal or possibly trying to get out of their mortgage, but it's also reported they turned down a lucrative offer by the *National Enquirer* to tell their story. What really happened on Larabee Street—a genuine paranormal encounter or a sensational story spun out of control—is unknown. The house still stands, with no known further encounters.

Ridgeway: Ridgeway Ghost

One of Wisconsin's oldest ghost stories comes from Ridgeway, a small town of about 637 people. Ridge Road connected people from Ridgeway to Dodgeville, Mineral Point and other cities in southwestern Wisconsin. By the 1840s, stories were circulating of a mischievous and sometimes violent ghost that tormented settlers and travelers along this stretch of road. In particular, there was a notorious stretch west of Ridgeway on Ridge Road (now Highway 18) known as the "Haunted Grove." Ridge Road was a thoroughfare for immigrant miners, many of them Welsh, Irish and Cornish. The road was dotted with farms and saloons. Stories of the Ridgeway Ghost or Ridgeway Phantom were passed down locally for generations.

What the ghost looked like differed from storyteller to storyteller. It appeared as a ghostly man walking down the road, and in other variations, the spirit is seen riding a phantom carriage drawn by two white horses. Sometimes it also appeared as a goat, a headless horseman or a hellhound with two glowing red eyes.

Folklorists have recorded hundreds of stories about the Ridgeway Ghost. Researchers Robert E. Gard and L.G. Sorden collected several of these in their 1987 book *Wisconsin Lore*.

One of the classic Ridgeway ghost stories involves a Welshman who encounters the ghost and takes off running as fast as he can. After running quite a distance, he sits down on a log to catch his breath, when a voice says, "That sure was some fine running!" When he sees that the ghost is now sitting next to him on the log, he replies that the apparition could expect to see more running as he leaps to his feet and takes off again.

In another story, a farmer reported that the ghost took over his water pump and began to pump enthusiastically, filling a tub and taking a drink from it. As the frightened farmer watched from his house, the ghost guzzled the water, turning into a blob-like shape.

Gard and Sorden also report an encounter between three men playing poker in a saloon and a ghost. A phantom hand began to deal cards, and the men noticed a fourth empty chair was now occupied by a stranger they'd never seen who had his hat pulled down over his face. This stranger had some supernatural tricks—when a player would try to reach for a card, it would fly into the air, and soon the deck was orbiting around the table. The frightened players fled the bar, the bartender hid behind the bar drinking his stock and the ghost and the pot of poker money disappeared into the night.

The Ridgeway Ghost haunts the town's water tower. *Megan Helwin.*

The most shocking Ridgeway Ghost story appeared in the *New York Times* on December 7, 1902. In this article, the spirit is blamed for beating a man to death. The paper noted that John Lewis was "a prosperous farmer living in the vicinity of Ridgeway, a man of sober life, and undaunted courage." Lewis was taking a shortcut home one night when he encountered the ghost. He was found semi-conscious by a neighbor the next morning and claimed that he had been pummeled, crushed and thrown with cyclone-like force. He died a few hours later, but before he passed, he asserted "with his dying breath that he had come to his end by a supernatural agency," according to the article.

As the legend of the Ridgeway ghost grew, local pranksters took advantage of superstitions about the spirit to get one over on people. Stories of oxen hitched to carts the wrong way, stampeding horses, loose carriage wheel pins and drunks frightened by a ghost saying "boo" are more likely pranks caused by mischievous humans than actual ghosts. There's a classic Ridgeway tale of a prankster covering himself in flour and frightening people around town—until he met an old farmer who chased him with a shotgun. Some say that the spirit left the Ridgeway area after the railroad was built, with one report saying the ghost was spotted leaving town, riding on the steel cowcatcher on the front of a train.

The stories are not forgotten in Ridgeway, where a cartoon ghost decorates the water tower. Besides Halloween celebrations in Ridgeway, the ghost is the mascot of the annual "Run and Party with the Ghost" celebration, which takes place on Labor Day weekend, with runners sporting T-shirts bearing the apparition, followed by a day of food and activities.

TWO RIVERS:
GHOST OF THE CHRISTMAS TREE SHIP

Not all ghosts are apparitions of people. The legend of the Christmas Tree Ship begins with Captain Herman Schuenemann, aka Captain Santa, born in 1865 in Algoma, Wisconsin. Captain Schuenemann started an annual tradition of loading up his ship, the *Rouse Simmons*, with Christmas trees harvested in Michigan every November. He would make his way down to Chicago, where the "Christmas Tree Ship" had a joyous reception. Captain Schuenemann's ship was not the only one that delivered trees, but it became the most tragically famous.

Chicagoans eagerly awaited the arrival of the ship so they could board and pick out a tree. A reporter noted that in Chicago, "Christmas season didn't really arrive until the Christmas Tree Ship tied up at Clark Street." Captain Schuenemann was generous and had a great love for Christmas, so much so that he gave free trees every year to churches, poor families and orphanages.

Captain Schuenemann was aware that it was a dangerous job—his older brother, Captain August Schuenemann, had died in November 1898 delivering Christmas trees to Chicago when his boat, the *S. Thal*, sank in a terrible storm. Herman decided to carry on the legacy, bringing a cargo of trees that same year.

The *Rouse Simmons* had been built in Milwaukee in 1868, with the captain buying a share in it in 1910. The ship's final voyage began in Manistique, Michigan, where Captain Schuenemann loaded up as many evergreens as he could, more than five thousand trees. He tied some to the masts and rigging and began the three-hundred-mile voyage to Chicago.

There were allegedly a few bad omens. Several sailors quit before boarding, with one reporting a "lurking terror" that made them decide not to step onboard. Other superstitions included the ship departing port on a Friday and rats supposedly seen deserting the boat before it set sail from Manistique. The captain's crew also totaled an unlucky number thirteen.

One sailor had a less supernatural explanation, reporting that the boat's cargo was overloaded, and the schooner—then forty-four years old—was not in prime shape.

November 23, 1912, was a violent night on the lake. Several ships around Lake Michigan were lost. The winds howled, ice froze to the *Rouse Simmons* and ripped the sails and heavy waves thrashed against it. The ship's steering wheel was ripped from the boat. The Christmas Tree Ship, cargo and crew,

Last known photo of the *Rouse Simmons*, taken in 1912 as it entered the port of Waukegan, Illinois. *Great Lakes Marine Collection of the Wisconsin Marine Historical Society and Milwaukee Public Library.*

sank into the cold, dark lake off the shore near Two Rivers, Wisconsin, in an area nicknamed the "graveyard of the lake" because of the large number of shipwrecks in the vicinity.

A message in a bottle washed up in Sheboygan with a note that read, "Friday. Everyone goodbye. I guess we are all through. Sea washed over the deckload Thursday. During the night, the small boat washed over. Ingvald and Steve fell overboard Thursday. God help us. Herman Schuenemann." Some have suggested that this message might have been fabricated. But real evidence—the Christmas trees that were the ship's cargo—washed ashore for years to come.

Rather than deterring his family, Captain Schuenemann's wife, Barbara, and his daughters Elsie, Pearl and Hazel continued to run the Christmas tree shipping business, even doing a tree run that same winter. "Girl Captain to Brave Lake that Killed Father," a headline in the *Chicago Daily Journal* read on December 9, 1912, reporting on Captain Elsie Schuenemann taking over the business. The paper noted that as a child, Elsie "played with boats, not dolls." The Schuenemanns delivered Christmas trees to Chicagoans into the 1930s, when railways and road transportation took over as the primary tree business delivery method.

Scuba divers discovered the wreck of the *Rouse Simmons* in 1971, describing finding trees, stripped of their needles, still in its hold. A fishing crew found the ship's helm at a different location. Rogers Street Fishing Village Museum in Two Rivers has several artifacts recovered from the boat on display.

It's said that the *Rouse Simmons* still sails Lake Michigan. Just when the phantom ship appears varies from story to story—some say the twilight mists of November or during violent storms or on Christmas Eve or Christmas Day, sailing the choppy waters and still hoping to make it through the wind and deliver its cargo of Christmas trees to Chicago.

"Floating in the air…hazy, ice-laden, misty, white" is what the apparition looks like, according to one witness. It's said that if you are in another boat and spot the ghost ship, it is a bad omen for your ship—perhaps yours will be next to sink to a watery grave.

VERNON COUNTY: KICKAPOO POLKA BAND

The polka is the official state dance of Wisconsin, and there's a ghost story that is associated with this style that arrived in the state with European immigrants. In his book *Driftless Spirits: Ghosts of Southwest Wisconsin*, Dennis Boyer collected ghost stories, including one about a ghost polka band called the "Kickapoo Polka Band," also known in some spots as "The Dutchmen." The ghost group fills the night with polka tunes, but those who attempt to track the music down are led to a dead end. The music lasts anywhere from minutes to hours. The eerie polka has been heard in areas of Vernon County along the ridges of La Farge and Ontario, as well as Potts Corners and Viroqua.

One writer said that he listened to the ghost music near Billings Creek on the south side of Wildcat Mountain. "It sounded like a polka tune with some eerie quality of being echoed through the trees from quite a distance," Matt Johnson wrote for the *Vernon County Broadcaster* in 2012. "After a few minutes of this, the sound faded into the wind rushing through the trees."

The band has reportedly been able to play a wide range of polka styles, mostly instrumental, although Boyer reported that singing in different languages and yodeling sometimes accompanies the music, as does the sound of phantom feet dancing on a wooden floor. The music comes from woods, hillsides, valleys and spots where old barns used to stand.

Marshfield: Wood County Insane Asylum

Ghost stories and urban legends are often attached to abandoned insane asylums around the country. There are a lot of horrific details to work with—some standard practices in asylums included heavy restraints and sedatives, electroshock therapy, isolation and submerging patients in ice water as remedies to their mental illness.

Wood County Insane Asylum in Marshfield, Wisconsin, was a facility like this. The former asylum has mostly been demolished and is now the site of the Marshfield Scrap Company. The asylum was built in 1909 on a 640-acre site, the west wing of the facility having been designated for male patients and the east for women. A tunnel under Highway A led from the asylum to a farm, where patients performed chores and grew their own fruits and vegetables.

The institution was shut down in 1974 and relocated, and demolition of the old structure the housed the facility started in 2005. Although most of the buildings are gone, a few remnants remain standing, like a large stone barn and the tunnel.

Ghosts on the property include those of a couple of people who were supposedly killed in the tunnel under Highway A, including a young girl with long, dark hair and a patient who worked as an assistant in the boiler room and who is rumored to have seen the devil's face in the boiler fire and jumped in after it.

Another asylum with a haunted reputation is the Sheboygan County Comprehensive Health Center, commonly referred to as the "Sheboygan Asylum." Built in Sheboygan Falls in 1940, the facility operated in some capacity until 2002. Paranormal investigation groups have reported ghost activity like disembodied voices and footsteps. In 2016, four people hoping to have a ghost encounter were arrested for breaking and entering. An investigation of the Sheboygan Asylum was featured on the Destination America channel show *Destination Fear* in 2020.

West Bend: Old Courthouse Museum

The tallest building in West Bend is the eight-story former Washington County Courthouse, now home to the Washington County Historical Society's research center and museum. As J. Nathan Couch explained in his book *Washington County Paranormal: A Wisconsin Legend Trip*, the courthouse is also supposedly home to a ghost named George, a former custodian who was struck by lightning. George is identified by his janitor jumpsuit and a large ring of keys. He likes to hang around the basement stairwell. Couch discovered that the custodian's name was Waldemar Bernhagen (nicknamed "George") and that he had been injured when lightning traveled to the basement where he was working. Waldemar died about a year later, in 1939, due to complications related to the lightning strike.

In addition to George, a "black shadowy mass" has been spotted and phantom footsteps have been heard inside the building. A story about a suicidal person hanging themselves from the courthouse tower appears to be an Internet urban legend. The Washington County Historical Society offers "Haunted Museum Tours," with guides sharing the building's history and ghost stories, as well as the nearby Old Sheriff's Residence and Jail, supposedly haunted by the victim of a murderous sheriff.

MADISON: ORPHEUM THEATER

Old theaters seem to be a favorite place for ghosts to haunt, as we have numerous tales of paranormal activities at such locations, including the Modjeska, Pabst and Riverside Theaters in Milwaukee, as well as the Majestic and Barrymore Theaters in Madison.

Madison is also home to the Orpheum Theater, the most haunted place in the capital city, according to Lisa Van Buskirk of Madison Ghost Walks. Orpheum is a common theater name from this period (there are also haunted Orpheum Theaters in Sioux Falls and Memphis). The name is a reference to Orpheus, the tragic Greek champion of poetry and music, who traveled to the Underworld in search of his love, Eurydice.

The Orpheum is located about a block away from the Capitol Building on State Street, where its giant sign is a landmark. Built in 1926, the limestone Art Deco building is richly detailed with a grand staircase and chandeliers. The Orpheum originally staged vaudeville performances and was later turned into a movie house.

An arsonist almost burned down the Orpheum Theater in 2004, and the building fell into a state of disrepair. It got a major restoration in 2013, however, and retains many of its original features. It is a popular venue for live music and comedy.

The Orpheum Theater. *Author photo.*

An entire staff of ghosts has been identified as those who haunt the Orpheum, including a spirit called the "night manager," a former employee whose footsteps and jangling keys are heard as he roams the theater in the twilight hours. Strains of ghostly dialogue between two people who aren't present have been reported. There's also a well-dressed woman who looks like she's from the 1930s who has been seen hanging out near the theater's side entrance, as well as the ghost of a child who appears as a red mist. The spirit of an usher, who reportedly met his demise upon falling from the balcony, is another of the otherworldly residents and has been seen attending the theater and hanging out by the soundboard.

A spirit named Projectionist Pete lurks in the projection booth and regularly relocates items. The legend says that Pete committed suicide and now haunts the theater. Van Buskirk related a story to the Madison college newspaper, the *Badger Herald*, about a manager who asked the ghost to leave them alone upon finding a mess in the projection room. Van Buskirk said that the manager felt hot breath on his face in the quiet room and proceeded to run downstairs to the bar area, where he heard a crash and found a pile of dishes that had been knocked to the floor, presumably by an angry spirit. People have also described feelings of intense fear in the furnace room and the area by the lower-level restrooms.

MANITOWISH WATERS: LITTLE BOHEMIA LODGE

Wisconsin's Northwoods were an escape destination for Chicago gangsters looking to lie low and cool their heels for a while, and the Little Bohemia Lodge was the scene of one of the best-known chapters in gangster history: the violent and chaotic 1934 shootout between the Dillinger Gang and the Federal Bureau of Investigation.

Located off Highway 51 near the town of Manitowish Waters, the Little Bohemia Lodge was built in 1929. On April 20, 1934, the Dillinger Gang—John; Lester Gillis, aka George "Baby Face" Nelson; Homer Van Meter; Tommy Carroll; John "Red" Hamilton; Nelson's wife, Helen; and three of the gang members' girlfriends—all checked into the lodge. Lodge owner Emil Wanatka's wife told someone that the Dillinger Gang checked in, and the tip was passed on to the FBI, who flew up from Chicago. The overzealous agents opened fire on innocent bystanders, whom they mistook for the gangsters, alerting Dillinger and his associates to their presence. Nelson shot

Little Bohemia Lodge. *Chad Lewis*.

back at the agents, and all the gang members escaped through the back door into the woods while the FBI continued to fire on the lodge. It was an embarrassing episode for the FBI that left one agent and one innocent bystander dead and other agents and customers wounded, while the gang stole vehicles and left unscathed.

The lodge is still open to the public to this day. You can see some remaining bullet holes from the incident in the windows and walls, as well as a collection of memorabilia from the shootout and the 2009 biopic *Public Enemies*, which was filmed on location at the lodge and stars Johnny Depp as Dillinger.

The ghost stories of shadowy figures and mysterious noises on the grounds are attributed to the innocent bystander or FBI agent who died in the shootout, although some say it's Dillinger's ghost who haunts the lodge. That's quite a distance from where Dillinger later died, at the Biograph Theater in Chicago in 1934 after he was shot there, but figures like Al Capone and John Dillinger are so much larger than life that they are said to haunt multiple locations.

OSHKOSH: GRAND OPERA HOUSE

A real phantom of the opera might have made a location in Oshkosh his otherworldly home. The Grand Opera House (now called the Grand Oshkosh), at the intersections of High Avenue and Market Street, opened on August 9, 1883, with a production of a famous opera of the time, *The Bohemian Girl*. After its initial use as an opera concert hall, the location played host to traveling road shows, vaudeville and then motion pictures.

Many legendary figures have graced the stage, including Harry Houdini, Mark Twain, the Marx Brothers, Charlie Chaplin and even Susan B. Anthony, who gave a speech at the venue.

The theater sunk into decline in the 1970s, becoming an X-rated movie house before finally closing. Fundraising and restoration work began, and the space reopened in the late 1980s, which is also when reports of supernatural activity started. The opera house got a major refurbish in 2009–10 and today hosts a variety of concerts and performances.

Some of the reported activity has included self-slamming doors, mysterious footsteps and disembodied voices. An actor in the 1980s recalled an encounter in his dressing room with an apparition of a man in old-fashioned clothing holding a playbill from 1895 in his hand.

The Grand Oshkosh, built in 1883 as the Grand Opera House. *Jennifer L. Bowen.*

Most of the theories about the suspected spirit haunting the opera house say it is Percy Keene, a former stage manager of the theater. Those who have seen the ghost identify it as Keene from his haircut, white shirt and small, round glasses. His specter has been reportedly seen hanging out in the opera house balcony, sometimes watching actors as they rehearse or peering out a second-story window on High Street.

Another ghost in the building is supposedly a mischievous young stagehand who died falling into a coal bin and now passes his otherworldly free time playing pranks on people. The dressing room mirrors are also said to be portals to a ghostly world, as people have spotted strangers in them out of the corner of their eye, but when turning around to confront the vision, they find they are alone. A phantom dog and a strange orange mist on the stage have also been spotted.

The opera house has undergone several paranormal investigations over the years and was featured in the 2017 documentary *Haunted State: Theatre of Shadows*, which explores haunted theaters in Wisconsin.

SPOOKY BREW: HAUNTED PUBS

For better or worse, "tavern culture" is strong in Wisconsin. Milwaukee was founded on the brewing industry, home to Pabst, Schlitz, Blatz and Miller, as well as a new wave of microbrewers that have popped up in the last few decades.

Many Wisconsinites spend spare time in bars and taverns around the state, and bars are often community centers for meetings and celebrations. It's not much of a surprise, then, that many establishments are said to be haunted by former owners or infamous guests. Here's a look at five Wisconsin bars that are supposedly haunted.

Baraboo: Old Baraboo Inn

Located in a former brothel and saloon, this tavern, more than 150 years old, was remodeled and reopened by entrepreneur B.C. Farr after sitting vacant for years. Farr and several other witnesses have identified ghosts frequenting the saloon, including one called "The Cowboy" and another who is a former saloon dancer. The Old Baraboo Inn is one of several bars that has embraced ghost tourism, offering paranormal-related presentations, workshops and tag-along investigations, visits from mediums and even a special shot called a "Ghost Bomb."

The Old Baraboo Inn. *Ben Wydeven.*

Madison: Wonder Bar Steak House

Built in 1929, the Wonder Bar was operated by Eddie Touhy, brother of Chicago gangster Roger "The Terrible" Touhy, a rival of Al Capone's. Many infamous gangsters hung out there, including members of the Dillinger Gang. Turrets in the building are said to have been built for Tommy guns, and the FBI surveilled the tavern. A tunnel led from the bar to Lake Monona to help in bootlegging operations. A ghost of a man in a trench coat and fedora has been spotted, and a sultry portrait of an unknown woman in a see-through negligee above the fireplace is said to be mystical and depicts one of the ghosts who calls the establishment "home."

Milwaukee: Pabst Properties

One of the brewers associated with the most ghostlore is Captain Frederick Pabst, who died in 1904 after establishing himself as one of Milwaukee's most successful beer barons. His ghost has been spotted at some of his old haunts in Milwaukee. A contractor working on remodeling Captain Pabst's historic Pabst Mansion (which is now a museum restored to appear as it did when the Pabst family originally lived there) spotted his ghost, as did an usher at the Pabst-commissioned Pabst Theater who saw Captain Pabst smoking backstage. His spirit is also suspected of haunting the buildings of the Pabst Brewing Complex, which produced beer until it shut down in 1996. The former structures have since been remodeled into bars and restaurants, venues and a hotel.

Milwaukee: Shaker's Cigar Bar

Another bar and former brothel that openly markets its ghost stories, this beautifully preserved bar is a place to get a meal and drinks, puff on cigars and have a paranormal experience. The bar offers tours of the building, and Hangman Tours offers other walking tours of the surrounding area. There's a Ghost Ale on tap, as well as frequent tarot card readers and séances that channel the spirits said to be inhabiting the bar, including former prostitutes and a little girl that hangs around the women's room.

Franksville: Brossman's Bar

In Franksville, a small town close to Racine, Brossman's opened in 1899 on what is now County Highway H. It was a saloon before Brossman's took over, dating back to the 1840s, a time before Wisconsin was a state. Stagecoaches would stop and hitch up so people could come in for a drink.

Some of the ghosts spotted include a little girl in a red dress, a woman in a white gown and a man in a cheap suit. Helen Brossman, former proprietor of the bar, said that she saw the ghosts and apparently has become one herself after her death in 2010. Spinning chairs, the TV turning on by itself, ghostly footsteps, doors shutting and paper towel dispensers shooting out towels are all among the claimed paranormal activity.

Wisconsin Dells: Captain Brady's Showboat Saloon

Captain Brady's Showboat Saloon is a colorful establishment on Broadway in the Wisconsin Dells that thrives on summer tourist business. A soul named Molly, who once lived above the saloon (and allegedly died there), is said to still haunt the upper level of this building, where she closes doors and plays with appliances in the early morning hours. In the bar, people have experienced ghosts in period clothing seen in the mirrors, disembodied voices heard near the stage and cold spots passing through them at the bar.

PART V

URBAN LEGENDS

U rban legends help give character to our creepy back roads, abandoned buildings and other unusual locations. Interestingly, urban legend tropes repeat themselves in locations across the country. In the ghostlore chapter, we discuss the Phantom Hitchhiker of Highway 12, a common legend. Many "Lover's Lane" stories revolve around a monster, ghost or deformed killer that haunts the moonlit roads, looking for lovers making out in their car to prey on, like the Goatman legend of Hogsback Road. Urban legends usually include an associated dare or ritual, such as turning car headlights on and off at a certain point, repeating an entity's name (saying "Bloody Mary" five times while looking in a mirror, for example) or trespassing onto spooky property.

Some urban legends are, unfortunately, at the expense of someone who is seen as an outsider and not "normal" and thus labeled as a supernatural ghoul. One of the urban legends you'll read about here is the "Witch's House," which was occupied by an artist who decorated her property with eccentric sculptures and was labeled a "witch." Other urban legends about a cat lady, a ghost with no legs, a community of little people and other stories might have been inspired by people seen as "unusual" by their neighbors.

Here are some of Wisconsin's best-known places steeped in urban legend ritual. A warning: Trying to snoop around on many of these properties will end not with a supernatural encounter, but rather a trespassing ticket.

MARIBEL: HOTEL HELL

In Maribel, Wisconsin, a small town of about 380 people, there's a structure that earned the nickname "Hotel Hell." The actual name of the building was the Maribel Caves Hotel, a former hotel and therapeutic spa built in 1900. A bottling plant on the property produced mineral water. The hotel changed hands and became a tavern and hotel until a fire destroyed the interior of the building in 1985, reducing it to its limestone shell. Urban legend says that Al Capone himself ran a moonshine business out of the hotel during Prohibition, utilizing the mineral water bottling plant for alcohol production.

I wrote an article titled "Chasing the Ghost of Al Capone" because the famous gangster's ghost is one of the most frequently spotted specters in America. His spirit has been said to haunt the prisons he did time in, Mount Carmel Cemetery (where he's buried) and in the countless speakeasies he may or may not have owned or frequented. If bootlegged beer or moonshine ran through the place, the legend goes, Al Capone's ghost follows.

The remains of Hotel Hell, 2019. *Chad Lewis*.

The creepy, burnt-out stone building became a favorite spot for trespassing young people to engage with spirits (in this case, alcohol) and create stories about the cursed property. Some of the tales include lore like the building being burned several times on the same date, that a psycho hotel guest killed everyone in the hotel and then committed suicide, that the negative energy of the property attracted a coven of witches that opened a portal to hell and unleashed evil spirits and that underground passageways on the property still contain the hidden treasure of Al Capone or other gangsters.

"One of the main legends told that if you looked into the old well that sits in front of the building, you would see a portal to hell open up and try to swallow you in," wrote Chad Lewis, author and researcher of all things strange. "People swore they felt an intense heat rise and see flames rising from the well." Another claim, noted Lewis, goes that if you carried a book through the hotel wreckage, it would burst into flame.

There is no evidence to support any of the alleged history of the hotel. Those who have dared to sneak onto the property have reported hearing ghostly voices and screaming, objects levitating and seeing the ghost of a little boy who died in the fire; there was a dare that shining a light in the second-floor window would prompt a response of a light shining back or spotting ghost children in the window.

In 2006, the interior of the building was gutted, leaving just its stone walls. In 2013, a wind storm toppled quite a bit of the stone structure, leaving only a few scraps of "Hotel Hell" standing.

MUSKEGO: HAUNCHYVILLE

An urban legend trope you'll find repeated in various parts of the country is the story of a village of angry little people or creatures. There are urban legends from Michigan, Ohio and Connecticut about a group called the "Melon Heads" or "Wobbleheads," short humanoid creatures with bulbous heads that terrorize people who are unfortunate enough to enter the roads they haunt.

A teenage rite in Muskego (a suburb outside of the Milwaukee area) was driving down the mysteriously named Mystic Lane at night, past the "No Trespassing" signs, to find the secret town of Haunchyville. This urban legend dates back to the 1950s and says there is a hidden village with a population of little people, sometimes said to have been former circus performers. In some tellings, they rebelled against their cruel ringmaster, cutting off his arms and legs and hanging him from a tree.

The "Haunchies," as they're known, violently rejected the outside world and angrily confront those who try to visit. A series of small, dilapidated stone huts that used to exist there in an overgrown pocket at the end of the "No Trespassing" signs probably does the trick at night.

Over the years, the story has grown legs and run amok. Embellishments on the legend say that the Haunchies have an unusually tall albino bodyguard that wears overalls and is armed with a shotgun or axe, that the Haunchies will cut off your limbs at the knee if you dare enter or that they'll run after your car and throw bricks at it. Searching for the hidden village of angry little people made a late-night trip down Mystic Lane a ritual for people for decades, but the journey was more likely to end in a trespassing ticket than it was an eerie encounter.

When revisiting the Haunchyville story in 2015, *Milwaukee Record* reporter Matt Wild found something more disturbing than a Haunchy riot—the area said to be Haunchyville had been cleared and the land had been developed into yet another boring subdivision, the stone huts and brush removed to make way for giant lawns, crushing and homogenizing a beautiful urban legend.

STEVENS POINT: RED, BLACK AND BLOODY BRIDE BRIDGES

Stevens Point has several legends about bridges around town. To get a closer look, I spent an afternoon driving around the area with Valerie Kedrowski of the Stevens Point Paranormal Club, who has studied the lore surrounding Black Bridge, Red Bridge and Bloody Bride Bridge. The same ghost of a bride is sometimes said to haunt all three, her spirit flowing through the waterways underneath.

The Black Bridge, a steel bridge on the Wisconsin River, had construction finished by 1872. It has had a long history, including a fatal train crash in 1916 and a fire in 1925. The legend has it that you can spot a shadowy black mass lurking on the bridge or a woman in a white dress floating across it. The story is that this woman's husband died in a nearby mill accident, and she was so bereaved that she committed suicide on the bridge and is now stuck wandering the afterlife looking for her husband.

Bloody Bride Bridge in Stevens Point. *Valerie Kedrowski.*

Red Bridge can be found out on Casimir Road, a dirt and gravel lane named for its red metal guard rails. It's a short bridge that stretches over a creek and is a popular spot to go fishing. The legend is that if you stop in the middle of the bridge at midnight and turn off your headlights, the ghost of a woman (in some versions, the "Bloody Bride") will appear. In a variation, the legend says you need to park on the bridge, shut off your engine and flash your headlights three times, whereupon ghosts will try to push your car off the bridge, leaving their handprints on your vehicle.

The actual "Bloody Bride Bridge" is located on Highway 66 near Jordan Park in Stevens Point. The story goes that the bride was either killed in an accident or committed suicide on her wedding night on the bridge. Later, a police officer thought he had hit a woman on the road crossing it. He got out to investigate and found nothing, but when he got back in his car, he looked in his rearview mirror and saw the ghostly bride sitting in his backseat.

Now, if you, brave reader, stop your car on Bloody Bride Bridge (please don't cause an accident), it is said that you will see the ghostly bride staring at you from the back seat of your car in the rearview mirror. Some versions of the story say this will only occur if you do it at midnight. In any case, no research has discovered a bride who died on this bridge or an encounter reported by a police officer.

STEVENS POINT: BOY SCOUT LANE

Also from Stevens Point is the story of the country lane known as Boy Scout Lane. The road tapers off to an unpaved red dirt and gravel road that dead-ends near a field and a few houses. According to urban legend, this was the location of the gruesome mass murder of a Boy Scout troop. Like most good urban legends, you'll find a few variations on the details of the alleged incident. One version says the Scouts were hunted by their psychotic bus driver or Scoutmaster one by one and picked off, as in a slasher film. In other tellings, their bus driver murdered them in a mad frenzy, setting the bus or the forest they were camping in on fire, thereby killing the entire group. Other stories blame a lantern accidentally being knocked over as the start of a killer fire or the troop getting lost in the woods and dying from exposure to the elements.

No such gruesome incident happened, and the lane gets its name because the Boy Scouts of America purchased part of the land to turn into a camp that never came to fruition, leading to the abandoned road and field. That hasn't stopped the stories—the legends say that if you drive down the lane at night, you'll spot ghost lanterns, and handprints of children will appear on your car. As we cruised down Boy Scout Lane, Valerie told me that the residents living near the dead end of the road would sometimes prank trespassers by scaring them.

Close to Boy Scout Lane are a few other urban legend stories. Nearby Old Swanson Road or County Road II is where it is said you will see a

Boy Scout Lane. *Valerie Kedrowski.*

legless man holding a bouquet of flowers who will ask people passing by for directions to his wife's grave. It's said he is legless because he died in a train accident and now haunts the road he lived on. Valerie did some research and found an article from 1916 that reported on a Siebert Swanson, who died after being struck by a train, which probably spawned this legend. But Swanson was killed in Amherst, Wisconsin, approximately sixteen miles away.

Also in the same area is the small Woodville or Linwood Town cemetery, commonly called the Calvin Blood Cemetery. The legend is that an army deserter named Calvin Blood hanged himself from a tree in the graveyard. Other versions say it was his wife that was found hanging, but these stories aren't true. Blood was deployed twice in the Civil War and received a pension from the army, dying at age eighty-two from gangrene. His wife died a year later from heart disease. The legends perhaps started because of Calvin's last name, Blood. The cemetery has seen a sad amount of vandalism from bored local teens. The graveyard is now fenced off, and anyone approaching the lot is met by an enthusiastic caretaker who will advise you that you are trespassing unless you are a relative of the deceased.

CREEPY COUNTRY LANES: PARADISE ROAD, WITCH ROAD, JAY ROAD AND WEARY ROAD

Another eerie road that has long been a destination for those seeking an urban legend thrill is Paradise Road, a long, winding road that turns into a single lane surrounded by a thick growth of forest in Jefferson. There are a lot of eerie things going on out there, according to the legend. It's said you can see practitioners of black magick in the woods, mysterious figures in hooded monk robes. You'll see bodies hanging from the trees (sometimes only visible in your rearview mirror); some stories report that these are the ghostly bodies of hanged witches. There's a legend of a couple parked in their car out there that got stabbed to death. Decapitated zombie raccoons can be seen crossing the road, and anguished screams are heard in the night. People have also reported seeing a mysterious albino deer wandering around.

A similar story comes from Rosendale, a small community outside Ripon, where there is a Callan Road that has been nicknamed "Witch Road." After the death of a witch who lived on the road—you can still see her dilapidated shack—her spirit has haunted this stretch, along with a little girl ghost that peeks out at people driving by.

There are also a few stories about Jay Road, sometimes called "Seven Bridges Road," which stretches from the small town of Boltonville in Washington County and heads east to Ozaukee County and Lake Michigan. In his book *Washington County Paranormal: A Wisconsin Legend Trip*, author J. Nathan Couch shared the most famous story about Jay Road, which involves an urban legend of a vengeful cat lady. The tale says that a pack of vicious Boltonville teens harassed and tormented the woman's felines. This led to an escalating feud, with the teens eventually lighting the cat lady's house on fire while the woman and her pack of cats were asleep inside. The woman refused to leave her pets as they burned alive, but as she went up in flames, she put a curse on the land. Now her hideous, charred spirit wanders the road, looking for revenge. It's said you can see her burning ghost house as well as the apparitions of her cats roaming around.

The second Jay Road story is about "the jogger." Supposedly, a young woman was jogging outside Boltonville near a swamp area when she was struck and killed by a drunk driver. Now, as you're driving at night, you might spot fog rolling off the swamp that forms into the shape of a woman, who looks over her shoulder at you as you approach before she screams and dissipates into the night. Some versions of the story say you'll spot her in your back seat in the rearview mirror or that she will suck the power from your car battery.

Last, there is a legend about Weary Road, located in Evansville. Writer Jenna Buege tracked down the story for her website, The Peculiar Adventurer. It's said that on this country lane—surrounded by trees that Buege described as "thick, tall, and ghoulish"—an "Old Man Weary" preyed on children, so the community burned him alive in his home. To see Old Man Weary, you must drive down this road three times. On the third time, if you look in your car mirrors, you'll see him creeping toward you. Other stories say that if you turn off your headlights, your car won't restart, and if you get out of your car, you may be scratched by the angry spirit or witness ghost lights.

SIREN: SIREN BRIDGE

This urban legend from the village of Siren in Burnett County says that a family was driving on County Road B when the car skidded off the road over a small land bridge and overturned in the swampy stream below; the trapped family of three inside drowned. Sometimes the detail that the accident happened during a blizzard on Halloween is added.

People driving over the bridge allegedly hear the voice of a little girl saying, "Help me, mommy! I can't get out!" coming through over their car's radio.

Online message boards list the people who died in the accident as a Rick and Rose Kringle and their daughter, Jo Dee, with the date of the accident listed as March 3, 1985. A listing for Oak Grove Cemetery in Webster, Wisconsin, does register a Richard, Rose and Jo Dee as being buried there on March 7, 1985. A commenter on the message boards noted that their truck is said to have slipped on ice and flipped off the road. It looks like the accident did happen, but whether haunted voices can be heard on the radio waves on that stretch of road is up for debate.

APPLETON: THE GRAVE OF KATE BLOOD

This grave is located in Riverside Cemetery in Appleton. Obviously inspired by the last name, the legends say that the grave of Kate Blood is the final resting spot of an axe murderer (or a witch) buried by her husband, George, whom she had supposedly murdered, along with their three children, before killing herself. The tombstone lists Blood's short life as being from 1851 to 1874. It's said that those who approach her grave under a full moon will witness it oozing blood and might spot her apparition wandering the graveyard, sometimes reportedly with an axe in hand. Her grave is slightly removed from the other tombstones, and the legend notes that it was deliberately removed to set her aside from the general population of the graveyard.

In reality, "Kitty," as she was more commonly known, died of tuberculosis at age twenty-three, and her husband outlived her, later remarrying. Like the grave of Calvin Blood, the legends were probably invented based on her unusual surname.

Mysterious graves of this nature are a familiar ghost story trope. Noah Leigh of Paranormal Investigators of Milwaukee went to high school in Berlin, Wisconsin, where he explored a local legend about a grave, the

Grave of Kate Blood. *Shane Van Boxtel.*

headstone of which included an engraving of a hand holding a dagger on it, which is supposedly the final resting place of a man and one or more of the ex-wives he murdered. The knife would supposedly ooze blood, but Leigh found that the likely cause of the bloody color was rust caused by rain.

In Green Lake, Dartford Cemetery is supposedly haunted by the ghost of Chief Highknocker (1820–1911) of the Ho-Chunk tribe, named for his love of wearing a stovepipe hat. The chief's death certificate lists the cause of his demise as accidental drowning, and it's said he drowned in the nearby Fox River while attempting to swim across while drunk. The spirit of Chief Highknocker is supposed to shove off anyone who dares sit on a mausoleum near his grave in the cemetery. Ghost stories were probably inspired by Chief Highknocker's tombstone, which features a portrait of him etched on the stone that looks creepy due to weather having worn the portrait down to make him look like he has vacant, blank eyes and ghostly features.

FOX POINT: THE WITCH'S HOUSE

Although urban legends overall are just goofy fun, they also sometimes come at the expense of someone who doesn't fit into society, is considered eccentric or a loner. One case in point would be the urban legends surrounding the "Witch's House" in Fox Point, a suburb near Milwaukee.

The stories among neighborhood children were that an old witch lived in a house at the end of the street, a whimsical and artistic property that is filled with sculptures of cartoonish people and creatures all over the yard. These statues, the story went, were of people the witch had turned to stone. In some tellings, some of the sculptures were of the witch's family, who had drowned in nearby Lake Michigan, which the house overlooks.

The reality was that the home belonged to artist Mary Nohl, who never married or had a family of her own and lived alone, spending her time creating paintings as well as the statues decorating her property. Kids dared one another to sneak onto her lawn, and after her statues were repeatedly vandalized and her windows broken by trespassers, she was forced to put a fence around her property.

Milwaukee's favorite musical sons, the Violent Femmes, featured the property on the cover of the band's second album, *Hallowed Ground*.

The Mary Nohl Art Environment. *Rita Lange.*

After her death in 2001, Nohl's will generously left her money to the Greater Milwaukee Foundation, which administers an arts education program called the Mary Nohl Foundation and a Mary Nohl Fellowship, part of which is awarded annually to local artists. Her house, the Mary Nohl Art Environment, is now in the National Register of Historic Places.

There has long been a plan to open the property as a museum, but the Fox Point neighborhood hasn't been receptive to the project; one ambitious idea called for moving the entire property to the Kohler Art Center in Sheboygan. Museum ambitions have yet to come to fruition, but her estate is still maintained and you can peek through the fence at the strange menagerie of her life's work.

ELK MOUND TOWER

Mound Hill Park was built in the 1930s in Elk Mound, near the Minnesota border. It was built as a memorial to rural mail carriers. It features a twenty-five-foot-tall castle-like observation tower that has sweeping views of the area. Beneath the "castle" in the mound below it, children are told, is a slumbering dragon. It's also said that a ghost haunts the tower, with stories of disembodied screaming, laughter, appearances of strange lights and mists and intense feelings of fear. The tower might have gained a ghostly reputation from being closed for several years due to road problems in the park.

PHANTOM CLOWNS

During 2015–16, I ran an ongoing Facebook status called "Clown Watch," in which I shared news stories from around the world of a strange trend of people dressing up as clowns and creeping around at night. In most cases, these were pranks or hoaxes propagated on the Internet and people trying to scare other people with clown imagery. This evolved into rumor and Internet urban legend and turned into a "Great Clown Panic of 2016," which was often more hysteria than truth.

Wisconsin has quite a history of "phantom clowns," as they're sometimes called. Reports of these colorfully clad entities goes back to the 1980s, according to Loren Coleman, a cryptozoologist who has an interest in unusual phenomena. He first reported on phantom clowns in his book *Mysterious America*, initially published in 1983, in which he detailed a wave of phantom clown sightings. In 1981, Coleman noted, there was a wave of clown appearances that started in the Boston area, jumped to Kansas City and spread to other cities, including Omaha and Providence. The Kansas City encounters were particularly disturbing, as the clown spotted driving around in a yellow van was reportedly threatening children with a knife.

In an updated edition of *Mysterious America*, Coleman reported on a 2000 story covered by Madison's *Wisconsin State Journal* of a man dressed as a clown holding balloons who tried to lure children into the woods near the King James Court Apartments building in Fitchburg (a small town near Madison). He was wearing face paint and a white wig, with a red nose and shoes and yellow overalls. Police contacted local clown performers, all of whom were ruled out as suspects.

Another clown-related story, reported by podcast and website *Mysterious Universe*, comes from a man named Dan Mitchell, who claimed that he and his family were visited in the '80s (when he was a child) by an entity he called the Mysterious Harlequin, a supernatural being dressed in a clown costume. Mitchell claimed the Harlequin would visit him at night and talk, dance and act out theatrics, telling him that it was the Tooth Fairy. He continued to see the entity until his family moved from the house, but he reencountered the Harlequin in 2009, when he returned to the same Milwaukee suburb he grew up in.

Around 2015 and 2016, mystery clowns began to trend as a sort of prank or challenge, with people in clown costumes spotted around the world. One of the first cases was in July 2015, when someone in such an outfit was spotted in a Chicago cemetery. Clown mania exploded over the following year. In November 2015, a teenage boy was pranking Carroll University in Waukesha by dressing in a creepy clown mask and orange jumpsuit and lurking around campus.

At the height of the Great Clown Panic of 2016, as it became known, a Green Bay filmmaker named Adam Krause took advantage of the hype in a big way. He took a photo of his friend in a creepy clown suit holding black balloons under a bridge in Green Bay and posted it online in August 2016, pretending it was a random encounter. He was surprised to see how the photo went viral—media around the world shared the photo, reporting that the clown was stalking the streets of Green Bay, making plenty of people nervous about phantom clowns. Alarmed at how seriously people were reacting (including would-be clown hunters), Krause soon admitted that the photo was a publicity stunt for his short horror film *Gags*, a piece of art imitating life, that was released in October 2016.

After the *Gags* sightings in August 2016, copycats sprung up across the country and around the world. By October, the clown antics had snowballed to the point of getting out of control. People decided that they would use colorful costumes as part of their bad behavior. There was a report of a clown chasing people with a machete in Rhode Island, a man in a costume who attacked someone at Texas State University and a clown mob attack in Florida on Halloween. A residence hall at Merrimack College in Massachusetts was evacuated after reports circulated of an armed clown on campus. Many other cities reported people making threats online, and there were robberies and people brandishing weapons dressed in disguises. A Menasha couple was arrested for negligence after leaving their four-year-old home alone while they dressed as clowns to scare people.

Warning letters were sent home to parents, and the costumes were banned. Some costume store locations purged their stocks of clown-related outfits. As 2016 passed, so did the Great Clown Panic.

A full-length version of *Gags*, mostly filmed in Green Bay, followed in 2018. By then, the wave of sinister clowns running amok in the real world had, thankfully, subsided.

WAUKESHA: SLENDERMAN

Urban legends used to be shared around campfires, in school hallways and at sleepovers, but the Internet has become a new medium for spreading myths and hoaxes. In a case that shocked Waukesha and the world, on May 31, 2014, two twelve-year-old girls, Morgan Geyser and Anissa Weier, lured their friend Payton Leutner into the woods near a park after a sleepover. Once there, Geyser and Weier pushed Leutner to the ground and stabbed her nineteen times in an effort, they said, to impress an entity called Slenderman, a legendary character originally created for an online paranormal art contest.

In his definitive exploration of the subject, *The Slenderman Mysteries: An Internet Urban Legend Comes to Life*, author Nick Redfern explained the character's creepy appearance in those initial images in the online contest. Redfern noted that the photos

> *showed the tall, thin, black-suited and faceless Slenderman in the midst of groups of children. The creature also sported a number of octopus-like tentacles, which waved in the air and beckoned menacingly.…Thus, the Slenderman's infamously unhealthy and dangerous connection to kids and teenagers was born and unanimously accepted. Where there were children, there was sure to be Slenderman. In rapid-fire time, there was a new boogeyman in town.*

A new boogeyman, but one of familiar stock. As Redfern detailed, similar entities have been part of paranormal lore—there's old German folklore about a monstrous being called *Der Grossman*, which translates to "the Tall Man," who lurks in the Black Forest. Other similar entities include the mysterious Men in Black and depictions of extraterrestrials.

Slenderman spread virally as people created art, videos and short stories featuring the character. Many of these tried to blur the line between fiction and reality to make the stories scarier. Slenderman is an example of the new urban legends that emerge from the depths of the Internet and are shared with the click of a button.

Geyser and Weier absorbed the Internet stories of Slenderman, after which they devised their plan to ambush Leutner, sacrifice her as a tribute to the Internet monster and then walk to Nicolet State Forest (about two hundred miles away), where they believed they would be greeted and accepted to live in a secret forest kingdom led by Slenderman and become

An artist's depiction of Slenderman. *David Beyer Jr.*

what they described as "proxies," or initiates. Geyser was later diagnosed with schizophrenia, and in 2018, Geyser and Weier were both given lengthy sentences in mental health facilities. Their victim recovered from her wounds.

Among the theories presented in Nick Redfern's book is one that Slenderman is a form of demonic or ghost entity or a type of tulpa, which are entities said to be visions brought to life by the power of human thought. With the popularity of Slenderman online, the tulpa theory suggested, a mass will power brought him into our world.

Another example of an Internet urban legend is Momo, a creepy demon chicken lady (in actuality, it's a picture of a statue created by artist Keisuke Aisawa titled *Mother Bird*) that spread on the Internet, claiming that there was a dangerous "Momo challenge" online. This Momo entity was supposedly spreading games and subliminal messages spliced into videos of kids' shows like *Peppa Pig* on YouTube, encouraging young people to engage in violence against others or to commit suicide. Parents, panicked by the dangers of the Internet, fell for the hoax and spread it forward. But Momo, like Slenderman, is just another case of someone's creation taking on a life of its own online and getting blown out of proportion by some people.

LA CROSSE: SMILEY FACE KILLERS

I'm sure some people will dispute my inclusion of the Smiley Face Killers here as an urban legend, as they believe it to be fact, while others will label it a conspiracy. In any case, the Smiley Face Killers remain legendary, as no such individuals have ever been identified.

From forty to one hundred college-age white men have been found drowned in rivers, mostly in the Midwest and East Coast areas. The theory says these men are not victims of accidental drownings (usually paired with extreme intoxication) but have instead been picked off by a gang called the Smiley Face Killers, who drug and abduct them, kill them elsewhere and then throw their bodies into a river, leaving a graffiti smiley face symbol somewhere near the dump location.

The sites with the most alleged Smiley Face Killer cases come from La Crosse in the Mississippi River and Eau Claire in Half Moon Lake and the Chippewa River. The leading proponents of the theory are retired New York City detectives Kevin Gannon and Anthony Duarte, along with criminal justice professor Dr. Lee Gilbertson.

Although most of the alleged Smiley Face cases have been dismissed as accidental drownings, a 2002 case of a man named Chris Jenkins who went missing on Halloween in Minneapolis was different: it was determined, after evidence was reevaluated, that he had not jumped or fallen but had instead been thrown off a bridge.

However, criminal profilers, the FBI and several local law enforcement departments have shunned the Smiley Face Killers theory. They point to a more obvious cause of the deaths: extreme intoxication from binge drinking. La Crosse, as with many college towns, has a reputation for a heavy drinking culture, with one study ranking it as the sixth-drunkest city in the nation. In fact, it has more bars per capita than any other city in America. Smiley faces are commonly found graffiti, and spotting them near crime scenes is more likely coincidence than conspiracy.

Smiley Face Killers: The Hunt for Justice, a reality show that follows Detectives Gannon and Duarte and their research, included an episode chronicling the disappearance of Luke Homan, who vanished after a night of drinking in La Crosse in 2006. His death was ruled accidental.

Steven Spingola, a retired Milwaukee Police Department detective, doesn't believe the story has merit, as he outlined in his book, *Staggered Paths: Strange Deaths in the Badger State*. After reading more than one thousand pages of case files, his determination was that only three of the drownings had a criminal angle and the rest were suicides or accidents. "One thing is clear though: I can confidently state none of these men died at the hands of a serial killer," Spingola wrote in the conclusion of his book.

Others have an eerier theory—that a ghost in the river is responsible for the deaths. In the Wisconsin-made documentary *The Hidden Truth?*, director Scott Markus, along with researcher Jay Bachochin and his Wisconsin Paranormal Investigators group, team up with Neil Sanders, a retired chief deputy medical examiner of La Crosse, to investigate the drowning cases. In addition to the Smiley Face serial killer theory, they explored the "siren song theory," which suggests that a supernatural force spotted on the Mississippi River was leading the young men to their deaths.

PART VI
LEGENDARY PLACES

S ome places in Wisconsin haven't fit into any of the previous categories, but are legendary nonetheless, like the House on the Rock, or have several pieces of lore spread throughout a city, such as Whitewater. Here are some of Wisconsin's most unusual and noteworthy spots on the map.

WHITEWATER: SECOND SALEM

Whitewater is a small college town, the home of the University of Wisconsin–Whitewater, with a population of about 14,500, and it is full of stories of ghosts, witchcraft and other mysterious occurrences.

Much of the town's strange reputation dates back to when Whitewater was home to the world's first spiritualist school, the Morris Pratt Institute, which studied and taught spiritualism and psychic research. The school was named after Morris Pratt, a businessman who had moved from New York to Wisconsin as a young man in 1840. He was a devoted spiritualist for most of his life. In the 1880s, he met a well-known Wisconsin medium named Mary Haynes-Chynoweth, who told Pratt to invest money in land in northern Wisconsin. Pratt, the story goes, followed her advice and struck it rich in mining iron ore. Pratt had said that if he became wealthy, he would invest money back into spiritualism, which he did.

The Morris Pratt Institute opened in 1888 and had two sets of courses—one was a typical college curriculum like grammar, math and geography. The other set was directed toward aspects of spiritualism like mediumship and séances. Pratt called his institute the "Temple of Science." But to the local Whitewater population, the school seemed like a mysterious and eerie new neighbor on the corner of Center and Fremont Streets, and they nicknamed the new school the "Spook Temple."

It probably didn't help that the school was somewhat secretive. Many Whitewater residents didn't understand spiritualism and equated it to witchcraft, and Whitewater got the nickname "Second Salem" for its witchy reputation.

The Pratt Institute operated in Whitewater until 1946. The building was demolished in 1961. The institute moved just outside of Milwaukee to West Allis after it closed the Whitewater location, where it still operates and offers courses in spiritualism and mediumship.

The Second Salem reputation spun into many urban legends and supernatural stories. It's said that a supernatural vortex can be found inside the Witch's Triangle, an isosceles triangle that can be formed by connecting three cemeteries—Oak Grove (where it's said a witches temple was once located and now all the coven members and their altar are buried

The Morris Pratt Institute, 1889. *Wisconsin Historical Society, WHS-79802.*

The "Witch's Tower" on the UW–Whitewater campus. *Jackie Moran.*

somewhere in the graveyard), Hillside and Calvary Cemeteries. Everything inside the triangle is said to be haunted or cursed by witchcraft rituals. The Pratt Institute was located more or less in the middle of the triangle, and Morris Pratt himself is buried at Hillside.

There's a Whitewater urban legend of a character named Mary Worth, who varies in different tellings as an axe murderer, a witch or both; she rises on Halloween in one of the Witch's Triangle cemeteries (it differs, depending on who is telling the story) to stalk new victims.

There are a few stories about the UW–Whitewater campus that are passed down to incoming students as a sort of hazing ritual to try to spook them. The most well-known legend is that the stone water tower near Wells Hall is where witches traditionally carry out their black masses and has been nicknamed the "Witch's Tower." The Wells Hall dormitories are supposed to be haunted, and there is supposedly an ancient magic tome protected under lock and key in Andersen Library, written by the witches of Whitewater. This terrifying book supposedly leads whoever reads it to either commit suicide or get locked in a mental institute. Students are told that they will be expelled if they so much as ask to see it.

Lake Whitewater has stories about a lake monster or evil entity that dwells in the deep, some of which involve witchcraft used to awaken the beast.

A Whitewater establishment, Second Salem Brewery, celebrates this lore in both its name and in its brews, which are named after local legends. There's a Witchtower Pale Ale; Bone Orchard IPA, which celebrates Second Salem Brewery's location at the base of the Witch's Triangle; and the Beast of Bray Road Amber Ale, which celebrates the monster in nearby Elkhorn.

Black River Falls: Wisconsin Death Trip

Black River Falls got some notoriety as having a strange path due to a book and documentary called *Wisconsin Death Trip*. Although several other cities are mentioned, most of the photos and stories in the book center on Black River Falls from the 1880s through the early 1900s.

The 1973 book, by Michael Lesy, features photos, mostly taken in Black River Falls from the late nineteenth century by photographer Charles Van Schaik, accompanied by local news stories of the same time that document crime, disease, ghost sightings and mental illness as Black River Falls began to expand.

"Tramps are overrunning Grant County, raiding sheep and stealing horses. The farmers are organizing a vigilance committee," reads one entry from 1886.

Another report, from 1891, reads, "Mrs. John Larson, wife of a farmer living in the town of Troy, drowned her three children in Lake St. Croix during a fit of insanity. Her husband, on finding her absent from the house, began a search and found her at the lakeshore....2 of her children lying in the sand dead. The third could not be found. Mrs. Larson imagines that devils pursue her."

The book leaves you with the distinct impression that Wisconsin of the late 1800s was a strange and sometimes dangerous place to be. A docudrama film version of the book was released in 1999, directed by James Marsh and narrated by Ian Holm.

WISCONSIN'S UFO CAPITAL OF THE WORLD... ALL THREE OF THEM

Wisconsin has a long history of UFO sightings, from the genuinely mysterious to the hokey. A classic Wisconsin UFO case involves a farmer who says a UFO landed on his property and that the extra-terrestrial occupant gave him the gift of pancakes.

On April 18, 1961, Joe Simonton claimed that a silver craft landed on his property in Eagle River, Wisconsin, and that three strange humanoids exited the spaceship and began communicating with him by making gestures. He determined that they wanted water, so he brought them some, and in exchange, the visitors gave him three small pancakes, which Simonton described as "tasting like cardboard." As silly as the story sounds, the air force did investigate.

Incidents in three other Wisconsin towns led them to claim to be the UFO capital of our state, and each has its own annual celebration.

First up is Elmwood, the oldest of the traditions. Its UFO Days first took place in 1978 after a series of UFO sightings in the area in the 1970s. Dozens of people spotted them, including an officer who reported seeing a UFO at Kraemer's Quarry. The sightings are commemorated with a sign on County Road S. There was even talk of building a UFO landing pad in the area as a tourist attraction.

Speaking of, Wisconsin resident Bob Tohak, a welder, did build a "UFO landing port" on his property in Poland, Wisconsin, near Green Bay. A banner on it reads, "We are not alone," with a green extraterrestrial on it smiling benignly.

Belleville, Wisconsin, is another contender for the title of UFO capital of the state. The town has its own UFO Day, held in October, that features a parade and other festivities like a craft show and "alien costume ball" commemorating the 1987 sightings of UFOs by several people.

Last but not least, on Long Lake is Benson's Hide-A-Way, on Highway 67 just north of Dundee in Campbellsport on the northern tip of Long Lake. This bar hosts an annual UFO Daze that has been held there every July since 1988. Inside the tavern, you'll find evidence in the form of photos snapped of UFOs, as well as some extra-terrestrial decorations.

A nominee for a fourth UFO capital of Wisconsin, if we need one, should be Sturgeon Bay in Door County. That's where Jim and Coral Lorenzen founded the Aerial Phenomena Research Organization (APRO) back in 1952. The Lorenzens were inspired after they, along with several others, sighted a UFO in the sky above Sturgeon Bay, which they approximated to be eight hundred feet in diameter. Many other UFO sightings have been reported around Door County over the years.

The Lorenzens coauthored classic books on the topic like *Flying Saucer Occupants* (1967) and *UFO: The Whole Story* (1969), among others. The Lorenzens' group was one of the first to study reports of UFOs, often called "flying saucers" back then, reporting their findings in a newsletter called the *APRO Bulletin*. APRO formed many chapters around the country (the Lorenzens moved around after Sturgeon Bay, eventually settling in Tucson, Arizona) until it disbanded in 1988 (after the Lorenzens died), with many of the members starting a new group called the Mutual UFO Network, which today is the largest UFO research group in the world.

Another celebration of "space invaders" of a sort happens annually in Manitowoc. On September 5, 1962, a twenty-pound chunk of the Russian Sputnik IV spacecraft crashed into the intersection of Eighth and Park Streets. A ring on the street marks the impact point, and a cast of the fragment is available at the Rahr West Art Museum. Manitowoc celebrates with a science fiction–themed Sputnikfest each September, a street fest that features food, music, trivia, costume contests and a "Miss Space Debris" pageant.

MOUNT HOREB: TROLL CAPITAL

"Troll Capital" Mount Horeb was founded by a mix of ethnicities, but by the late 1800s, the town had a large Norwegian population who brought Scandinavian folklore with them, although the troll identity associated with the town didn't arrive until much later. The creatures coincide with the opening of Open House Imports in 1976, a shop that specializes in souvenirs and knick-knacks imported from Scandinavia. The wooden troll carvings on its front lawn were such a hit with tourists that Troll Fever soon spread throughout the town. By the 1980s, "The Trollway" was being advertised, named in honor of a series of wooden troll carvings placed along Main Street.

Trolls, according to Scandinavian folklore, are magical creatures associated with nature, like fairies. They are often (but not always) depicted as being big, slow, strong and dim-witted. They are sometimes said to eat people and turn to stone in sunlight. Of course, the ones found in Mount Horeb are the cuter version associated with troll dolls and knick-knacks.

Statues on Mount Horeb's Trollway. *Ron Lutz II.*

Jorgen, mascot of Mount Horeb. *Ron Lutz II.*

Numerous gift shops sell troll- and Scandinavian-themed items, and trolls are a theme throughout town, decorating and lending their name to local businesses. A dentist's office has a statue of a troll holding a giant toothbrush, and you can get a beer at the Grumpy Troll Brew Pub. An annual Thirsty Troll Brew Fest beer sampling takes place, and at local events, you can find Jorgen, the town's troll mascot, who often makes a costumed appearance for photo ops.

THE HOUSE ON THE ROCK

The House on the Rock, located between Dodgeville and Spring Green, is one of the most unique places on Earth, and its creation has led to it becoming a legendary place. One story about it involves Wisconsin's most famous architect, Frank Lloyd Wright, sometimes called the "greatest American architect of all time."

Wright was born in the farming community of Richland Center, Wisconsin, in 1867. In 1911, Wright built a home and studio in Spring Green, Wisconsin, that he named Taliesin. Wright lived at Taliesin with his mistress, Martha "Mamah" Borthwick, after leaving his first wife. Living with his mistress was considered scandalous, but Wright was unashamed and didn't care who knew. When the press got a hold of the story, they referred to the property as the "Love Cottage."

In 1914, Taliesin was the site of a massacre. Wright was out of town working in Chicago when Julian Carlton, Wright's cook and servant, snapped. He had recently been fired for his strange, paranoid behavior. Carlton murdered Borthwick and her two young children with an axe, setting their bodies on fire and then set the building ablaze. Several workers had gathered at Taliesin for lunch, including draftsmen and construction workers. As they tried to escape the fire, Carlton attacked them, killing or fatally wounding four more people. Carlton tried to kill himself by ingesting hydrochloric acid, badly damaging his esophagus, but survived and was arrested, dying forty-seven days later of starvation while in custody.

Wright rebuilt the property, but it suffered another fire in 1925; he rebuilt again. After his death, the property was given to the Frank Lloyd Wright Foundation. Taliesin Preservation Inc. maintains the property and offers tours.

The House on the Rock is not far from Taliesin, and the supposed origins of the eccentric structure have a tie to Wright. The idea for the House on the Rock, so the story goes, began when Alex Jordan Jr., the architect behind the building, drove out to Taliesin to meet Wright sometime between 1914 and 1923 to show him his plans for a building he designed in Madison, the Villa Maria. Jordan was hoping to get the famous architect, whom he admired greatly, to give praise and approval of the design, but instead he was told, "I wouldn't hire you to design a cheese crate or a chicken coop." On his drive back home, Jordan visualized his odd house on the top of a spire as he angrily drove down Highway 23. If you'll forgive the pun, a Frank Lloyd *Wrong* had been born in Jordan's mind.

The carousel room at the House on the Rock. *J. Jason Groschopf.*

Of course, this story is likely a complete fabrication. The building opened as an attraction in 1959 and expanded over the years into a collection of fantastic rooms of weird dimensions.

The House itself is on a sixty-foot rock column, with an Infinity Room that juts out over two hundred feet from the house, with three thousand windows. Different displays include "The Heritage of the Sea," which features nautical items, including a giant model of a whale, and "The Music of Yesterday," a collection of automated music instruments that fill the House with music. Jordan sold the House on the Rock in 1988 to a friend who maintained and built new displays. Jordan died the following year, but the site is still a tourist attraction.

The unique architecture has also entered pop culture on occasion, most notably in Neil Gaiman's 2001 novel *American Gods*. Gaiman moved from the UK to the Wisconsin Northwoods in the 1990s, where he first began spotting roadside signs for the tourist attraction.

The House on the Rock plays a memorable scene in *American Gods* when a group of the Old Gods gets on the House on the Rock's carousel, which is billed as the "world's biggest indoor carousel." It has 269 animals and twenty thousand lights on it. The carousel transports the Gods to another realm for a meeting.

"Most people think I made it up, whereas in actual fact I just toned it down a bit so that people would believe it," Gaiman said in an interview published in a special edition of *American Gods*, adding his reaction visiting House on the Rock for the first and even second time was, "I just don't believe this place."

A television adaptation of the book aired its first season in 2017 on Starz. The House on the Rock scenes were shot on location, adding another layer of mythology to this strange and wonderful place.

COUDERAY: THE HIDEOUT

Chicago's most notorious gangsters had hideout spots they fled to when things got too hot in the city. The most notorious gangster of all time, Al Capone, had many hideouts in Michigan and Florida, but most impressive was his fortified retreat here in the Northwoods of Wisconsin near Couderay, Wisconsin (close to Hayward), called "The Hideout." It included a lavishly decorated two-story stone lodge, a guard tower and a lake, which was said to have been used for small planes to land on to be loaded up with bootleg booze on a dock. Everything was fortified and designed for defense and a quick getaway. The garage where Capone's car was kept had gun slits in the walls in case of a shootout with the law.

If Capone felt the heat was on in Chicago, he'd head north to the hideout. Many Wisconsinites in the Couderay area had stories—real, embellished or fabricated—about encounters with Capone. The gangster spread goodwill with fistfuls of cash and was reportedly fond of buying kids candy and handing them crisp $100 bills.

One story of lore involves a local pastor who was struggling to fund his church. He bravely crossed the lake in a boat and told a security guard that he wanted to talk to Capone. The guard led him into the Hideout, where he found Capone puffing on a cigar and playing poker. He pled his case to the gangster, who studied him carefully and then handed him a stack of cash and wished him luck. Capone's ghost is said to haunt many Wisconsin locations, although his final days were spent in Florida. He's buried at Mount Carmel Cemetery in Illinois.

Other gangster spots in the Wisconsin Northwoods include Mercer, where Al Capone's brother Ralph operated the Rex Hotel (and a tavern attached to it named Billy's Bar) until he died in 1974; Hurley, whose Silver Street district (full of bars and strip clubs) was popular with vacationing gangsters; and the Northwoods Pines Supper Club in Minocqua.

PLAINFIELD: THE STORY OF ED GEIN

One of the most infamously gruesome chapters in Wisconsin's history is the story of Ed Gein of Plainfield, who was convicted of two murders in 1957. Gein had killed tavern owner Mary Hogan in 1954 and hardware store owner Bernice Worden in 1957. When police arrived at Gein's farmhouse, they made a shocking discovery: he had grave-robbed several corpses and made clothing, furniture and other items from female human remains, which he spread throughout his farmhouse where he lived by himself. The case influenced writers of horror books and movies, the most famous of which are *Psycho* and *The Texas Chainsaw Massacre*. Gein was convicted of murder and spent the rest of his life in mental institutes in Waupun and Madison. He died in 1984.

Gein's 1949 Ford sedan, which he used in his grave robbing expeditions, was sold to sideshow proprietor Bunny Gibbons, who charged carnival-goers a quarter to see it.

Plainfield today is a stopping point for dark tourists, although you won't find Gein's gravestone in the Plainfield Cemetery (he was buried by his parents). After it was chipped repeatedly for souvenir pieces, the entire headstone was stolen in 2000 and taken on a punk music, art and oddities tour. After police recovered it in 2001, it was placed into storage at the County Sheriff's Department so it wouldn't get ripped off again.

Ghost stories about Plainfield now include spirits in the cemetery where Gein grave-robbed and is buried, as well as in the True Value (formerly Worden's) hardware store where Gein killed his last victim, Bernice Worden.

The case inspired a horror writer, Robert Bloch, who had spent much of his life in Milwaukee until he moved to the town of Weyauwega, about thirty-five miles from Plainfield. The Gein case was part of the inspiration for his best-known work, *Psycho*, published in 1959, which in turn was the basis for the Alfred Hitchcock 1960 film of the same name.

SAUK CITY: ARKHAM HOUSE

Robert Bloch had his first book published by Arkham House, a small publishing imprint that was started by Wisconsin writer August Derleth from his home in Sauk City. It was formed to keep the legacy of Derleth's friend horror icon H.P. Lovecraft, in print.

Derleth was a prolific writer in a wide range of genres. He got his first story, "Bat's Belfry," published in classic horror magazine *Weird Tales* in 1926 when he was just sixteen. After that, Derleth became a regular contributor of short stories to *Weird Tales* and other pulp magazines. Shortly into his writing career, he wrote to one of his favorite pulp storytellers, H.P. Lovecraft. They began corresponding with each other, and Derleth became part of the "Lovecraft Circle," a group of pulp writers who wrote to one another, sharing their work and writer woes. Through the circle, he met Robert Bloch, who was living in Milwaukee.

Derleth and Bloch had discussed subsidizing a trip to bring Lovecraft to visit Wisconsin, so Lovecraft could visit Bloch in Milwaukee and Derleth out at Derleth's home in Sauk City (which he called Place of Hawks), but it never came to pass. In 1937, Derleth got the somber news that Lovecraft was dead at age forty-six from complications, including malnutrition.

Derleth, along with fellow writer Donald Wandrei, founded the Arkham House imprint to publish the first collection of stories by Lovecraft, *The Outsider and Others*, in 1939. At the time, copies sold slowly. But today, Lovecraft is seen as one of the biggest names in American horror, perhaps second only to Edgar Allan Poe. His writing and characters, like the monstrous cosmic entity Cthulhu, have inspired countless horror writers, artists, moviemakers and game designers.

Derleth had a keen eye for speculative fiction writers. In addition to being the first publishers of Lovecraft (after the first collection, Derleth went on to publish all of Lovecraft's works and volumes of the author's correspondence), Arkham House released the first works by Robert Bloch (*The Opener of the Way*, 1945) and sci-fi great Ray Bradbury (*Dark Carnival*, 1947), as well as an early collection of work by Robert E. Howard, who created the character Conan the Barbarian.

Derleth died on July 4, 1971. Arkham House remained in the family and continued to publish speculative fiction. The August Derleth Society has existed since the 1970s and is dedicated to preserving Derleth's writing.

BURLINGTON VORTEX

The Burlington Vortex theory has mainly been propagated by Mary Sutherland, the former proprietor of Burlington's Sci-Fi Café, author of books like *Haunted Burlington, Wisconsin* and *Portals: Gateways to the Multi-dimensional Worlds*, organizer of the Burlington Vortex Conference and a guide who leads tours to investigate the vortex in a wooded area of Burlington. The vortex is described as a sort of spinning energy that causes time and space distortions, or a metaphysical gateway. In *Haunted Burlington, Wisconsin*, Sutherland wrote, "In a vortex area, such as what we have in Burlington, portals are created, which are doorways into these other worlds or dimensions. When this happens, time and space become distorted, and a lot of strange things can and do happen. One may step into a doorway leading into another dimension and never notice; at other times, it is quite obvious that you are not in the same place or the same time—and some people have stepped into them never to return."

Side effects of this vortex include experiencing a disoriented equilibrium, "time loops" (gaining or losing a few minutes or hours) and temperature fluctuation. These portals (known collectively as the Burlington Vortex) are attached to Native American effigy mounds, according to Sutherland, and open an entryway for ghost orbs, Bigfoot, the Beast of Bray Road and fairy folk to pass through into our realm. On her vortex tours, candies like M&Ms are left out as a gift for any fairies hanging around.

One of the stops Sutherland has explored is called Dead Man's Hill, farmland with an old cemetery, where twisted trees are pointed to as evidence of one of the portals to another realm.

ST. NAZIANZ

A small town of seven to eight hundred people in Manitowoc County, St. Nazianz has lore surrounding it that sounds like something out of an occult horror film. The town is said to be cursed by a heretic priest, Father Ambrose Oschwald, who arrived in Wisconsin in 1854, leading a Catholic mystic cult known as The Association.

In his quest to chronicle all things strange, Charlie Hinz, the editor of the website Cult of Weird, researched and visited St. Nazianz. He found a newspaper article that noted that Father Oschwald and his flock followed a "divine white hefer [*sic*]," which led them to St. Nazianz, which they named after Archbishop Gregory of Nazianzus aka Gregory the Theologian. Father Oschwald fell ill and died in 1873, yet as Hinz discovered, his body was still in remarkably good shape a few months after he died when his tomb was opened for examination.

"A priest by the name of Father Mutz, along with a group called the Oschwald Sisters, noted that his body had not decayed, and there was no odor of corruption," Hinz wrote. "Oschwald's eyes had sunken in, but his skin had a lifelike complexion, his hair and fingernails were growing. They washed his face and noted it served to give him an even more natural complexion."

In 1926, Father Oschwald's coffin was opened as he was moved to a new stone mausoleum, but as Hinz reported for Cult of Weird, those moving him "observed through a glass cover that Oscwald's corpse was still in remarkably good shape after 53 years. His skin had become shrunken and sallow, but his body and vestments were still very much intact."

Besides the cemetery, there is lore about St. Nanianz's Salvatorian Seminary, later known as JFK Prep. The abandoned school is rumored to be "haunted by the souls of kids who suffered at the hands of abusive nuns," Hinz wrote. The weird legacy of Father Oschwald and The Association still haunts this little village.

THE APOSTLE ISLANDS

A scattering of twenty-two islands located off the northern tip of the state in Lake Superior, the Apostle Islands are filled with strange, spooky stories of hauntings and curses.

The most populated of the Apostles is Madeline Island, which was inhabited for hundreds of years by the Lake Superior Chippewas. French fur traders arrived in the late 1600s and later founded what is now La Pointe, a small community of about three hundred people who live there year round. La Pointe is an entry point to the island, a popular summer tourism destination, with the Madeline Island ferry crossing from Bayfield on the mainland. The island's long history has led to ghost stories, especially about the La Pointe Indian Cemetery, the Madeline Island Museum.

Many visitors to Madeline Island also have fond memories of stumbling across a miniature "hidden village." The tiny stone buildings feature homes,

Devils Island. *Missy Bostrom.*

a stable, a church and a town hall. Also called a "fairy" or "Smurf" village, you can find the structures on a forest path near a large birch tree, but residents are secretive about the exact location, as it is on private property.

The story of the Ghost of Hermit Island, also known as Wilson's Island, two miles northwest of Madeline Island, is the story of William Wilson. The story goes that Wilson ran afoul of "King" John Bell, acting sheriff of La Pointe on Madeline Island in the 1840s. They agreed to have a fistfight, with the loser having to pack up and leave town. After fighting all day and eventually losing, Wilson set up his lonely outpost, where he made a living crafting barrels for the fishing industry. After noticing no smoke from Wilson's house for several days, a Native American couple, Benjamin Armstrong and his wife, who lived on nearby Oak Island, rowed over and found him dead on his kitchen floor in the early 1850s. The stories suggest that there was foul play, probably from someone looking for Wilson's rumored stash of money. Over the years, the island was visited by treasure hunters who had heard rumors of Wilson's secret loot. Other stories say that French soldiers hid silver and gold somewhere on the island, but there are no reports of any of it turning up.

In the 1900s, a resort was built on the island that was reportedly haunted by the spirit of the hermit, angry at the flux of noisy visitors. As Hugh E. Bishop noted in his book *Haunted Lake Superior*, Wilson got the last laugh as the resort was abandoned and fell into a state of ruin in the 1930s, and the island is now a protected area that bars future development, giving Wilson the peace and quiet he deserves.

Devils Island, the northernmost piece of Wisconsin land, according to native lore, is where Kitchie-Manitou, the great spirit, had imprisoned Matchimanitou, an evil spirit. When the surf is heavy, the waves pummeling the island's sea caves make an intimidating booming sound, which natives believed was the sound of the angry imprisoned evil spirit.

Long Island is the site where an Ojibwe war party attacked and killed a group of Fox warriors. In November 1886, the schooner *Lucerne* foundered, and all ten crew members died icy deaths just offshore; the area is now said to be home to their vagrant spirits. On Raspberry Island, a ranger who worked at the island's lighthouse said that she experienced supernatural antics like ghostly footsteps and doors that locked by themselves.

The city of Bayfield is located across the lake from the islands. The Apostle Island National Lakeshore Visitor Center in Bayfield, located in an old county courthouse, is supposed to be haunted.

SELECTED BIBLIOGRAPHY

Bair, Deirdre. *Al Capone: His Life, Legacy, and Legend*. New York: Doubleday/ Talese, 2016.

Barnouw, Victor. *Wisconsin Chippewa Myths & Tales and Their Relation to Chippewa Life*. Madison: University of Wisconsin Press, 1977.

Bechen, Brooke. "Eight Years Later, Iowa County Kangaroo Still a Mystery." *Dodgeville Chronicle*, March 7, 2013.

Bell, Devon. "Terrorizing Tower." devonbellauthor.wordpress.com.

Bishop, Hugh E. *Haunted Lake Superior: Ghostly Tales and Legends from the Mythical Inland Sea*. Duluth, MN: Lake Superior Port Cities Inc., 2003.

Boyer, Dennis. *Driftless Spirits: Ghosts of Southwest Wisconsin*. Madison, WI: Prairie Oak Press, 1996.

———. *Giants in the Land: Folktales and Legends of Wisconsin*. Black Earth, WI: Trails Books, 1997.

Bradley, Mickey, and Dan Gordon. *Field of Screams: Haunted Tales from the Baseball Diamond, the Locker Room, and Beyond*. Guilford, CT: Lyons Press, 2010.

Brown, Charles E. *Lost Treasure Tales: Some Wisconsin Lost Treasure Legends and Tales*. Madison: Wisconsin Folklore Society, 1945.

———. *Sea Serpents: Wisconsin Occurrences of these Weird Water Monsters in the Four Lakes, Rock, Red Cedar, Koshkonong, Geneva, Elkhart, Michigan, and Other Lakes*. Madison: Wisconsin Folklore Society, 1942.

Brown, Dorothy Moulding. *The Fighting Finches: Tales of Freebooters of the Pioneer Countryside in Rock and Jefferson Counties*. Federal Writers' Project, Folklore Section. Washington, D.C.: Works Progress Administration, 1937.

———. *Wisconsin Circus Lore, 1850–1908: Stories of the Big Top, Sawdust Ring, Menagerie, and Sideshows*. Madison: Wisconsin Folklore, 1947.

Brown, Michael, director. *Haunted State: Theater of Shadows*. 2017.

Buege, Jenna. "The Legend of Wisconsin's Weary Road." Peculiar Adventurer, February 21, 2017. https://jennabuege.wordpress.com.

Coleman, Loren. *Mysterious America: The Ultimate Guide to the Nation's Weirdest Wonders, Strangest Spots, and Creepiest Creatures*. New York: Gallery Books, 2007.

Collar, Jim. "Kate Blood: The Woman Behind the Urban Legend." *Post Crescent*, October 28, 2015.

Couch, J. Nathan. *Goatman: Flesh or Folklore?* Self-published, 2014.

———. *Washington County Paranormal: A Wisconsin Legend Trip*. Self-published, 2012.

Derleth, August. *The Wisconsin: River of a Thousand Isles*. Madison: University of Wisconsin Press, 1985. Originally published in 1942.

Edmonds, Michael. *Out of the Northwoods: The Many Lives of Paul Bunyan*. Madison: Wisconsin Historical Society Press, 2009.

Erickson, Randy. "Random Eruptions: Man Bat Tale Tops 2006 for Weirdness." *Lacrosse Tribune*, January 3, 2007. lacrossetribune.com.

Finding Bigfoot. "Brews, Brats, and Bigfoots." Season 9, Episode 8, February 19, 2017.

Foran, Chris. "Once Upon a Time, Kangaroo Sightings Were a Thing." *Milwaukee Journal Sentinel*, August 2, 2015. jsonline.com.

Gaiman, Neil. *American Gods: The Tenth Anniversary Edition*. New York: William Morrow, 2017.

Gard, Robert E., and L.G. Sorden. *Wisconsin Lore*. 12th printing. Ashland, WI: Heartland Press, 1987.

Godfrey, Linda S. *Monsters of Wisconsin: Mysterious Creatures of the Badger State*. Mechanicsburg, PA: Stackpole Books, 2011.

Godfrey, Linda S., and Richard D. Hendricks. *Weird Wisconsin: Your Travel Guide to Wisconsin's Local Legends and Best Kept Secrets*. New York: Sterling, 2005.

Hathaway, Aaron. "Behind the Curtain of Madison's Concert Venues, the Undead Put On Their Own Performances." *Badger Herald*, October 27, 2015.

Hintz, Charlie. "June 2019 Newsletter: The Flying Saucer Woman Who Changed UFO Research Forever." Cult of Weird, June 6, 2019. cultofweird.com

———. "St. Nazianz: Wisconsin Town Founded by Heretic Priest and Mystic Cult Followers." Cult of Weird, February 27, 2015. cultofweird.com.

———. "Tracking Down the Haunted Tallman House of Horicon, Wisconsin." Cult of Weird, June 29, 2015. cultofweird.com.

Jacobson, Brian. "Travel Channel Seeks City's Secret 'Treasure.'" Urban Milwaukee, October 7, 2013. urbanmilwaukee.com.

Johnson, Caitlin. "The Case of the Muskie: A Fish Story." CBS News, October 8, 2006. cbsnews.com.

Johnson, Matt. "Outsider: Eerie Close Encounters with Ghosts in Vernon County." *Lacrosse Tribune*, October 24, 2012. lacrossetribune.com.

Jornlin, Allison. "Major League Paranormal Activity at the Pfister Hotel." Milwaukee Ghosts Blog, July 13, 2010. mkeghosts.wordpress.com.

Kedrowski, Valerie. Interview with the author, May 9, 2019.

Kewaunee County Press. "Katoose, the Pottawattamie Chief, Recounts Legend of Ah-ne-pe, Great Wolf." December 8, 1923.

Kortenhoff, Kurt Daniel. *Long Live the Hodag: The Life and Legacy of Eugene Simeon Shepard, 1854–1923.* Savage, MN: Hodag Press, 2006.

Krulos, Tea. "Chasing the Ghost of Al Capone." Cult of Weird, October 11, 2016. cultofweird.com.

———. "The Horror of Sauk City: Arkham House's 'Weird Fiction' Legacy." Urban Milwaukee, October 30, 2013. urbanmilwaukee.com.

———. *Monster Hunters: On the Trail with Ghost Hunters, Bigfooters, Ufologists, and Other Paranormal Investigators.* Chicago: Chicago Review Press, 2015.

———. "Thus Concludes the Summer of the Lion." *Riverwest Currents*, September 2015.

Labeled (podcast). "The Rave in Milwaukee Is the Scariest Club in America." Season 1, Episode 13, October 24, 2017.

Leary, James P., ed. *Wisconsin Folklore.* Madison: University of Wisconsin Press, 1998.

Lesy, Michael. *Wisconsin Death Trip.* New York: Pantheon Books, 1973.

Lewis, Chad. "Hotel Hell." Unexplained Research, September 28, 2004. unexplainedresearch.com.

———. *Lake Monsters of Wisconsin.* Eau Claire, WI: On the Road Publications, 2016.

Lewis, Chad, and Terry Fisk. *The Wisconsin Road Guide to Haunted Locations.* Eau Claire, WI: Unexplained Research Publishing Company, 2004.

Loew, Patty. *Indian Nations of Wisconsin: Histories of Endurance and Renewal.* 2nd ed. Madison: Wisconsin Historical Society Press, 2013.

Madison.com. "Legend of Ridgeway Ghost Includes a Death." August 16, 2006.

Markus, Scott, director. *The Hidden Truth?* Documentary, 2014.

Meier, Allison. "Saving the Art and Home of Mary Nohl, Whose Neighbors Called Her a Witch." Hyperallergic, August 16, 2017. hyperallergic.com.

Milwaukee Magazine. "Behind the Midwest Smiley Face Killers" (October 27, 2008).

Monsters and Mysteries in America. "Mill Race Monster, Toxic Rain, Devil Dogs." Season 3, Episode 6, February 25, 2015.

Newkirk, Dana. "Welcome to the Summerwind Mansion: An Abandoned Hotbed of Demonic Possession." Roadtrippers, January 6, 2016. roadtrippers.com.

Offutt, Jason. "The Mysterious Harlequin." Mysterious Universe, November 23, 2011. mysteriousuniverse.org.

Pennington, Rochelle. *The Historic Christmas Tree Ship: A True Story of Faith, Hope, and Love.* West Bend, WI: Pathways Press, 2004.

Pressman, Stacey. "The Haunting of MLB's A-List." *ESPN Magazine* (May 31, 2013).

Redfern, Nick. *The Slenderman Mysteries: An Internet Urban Legend Comes to Life.* Newburyport, MA: Weiser, 2018.

Roadside America. "Sputnik Crashed Here." roadsideamerica.com.

Sheboygan Press. "Four Search for Ghosts, Find Criminal Charges." May 13, 2016.

Smallman, Shawn. *Dangerous Spirits: The Windigo in Myth and History.* Victoria, BC: Heritage House, 2015.

Smiley Face Killers: Hunt for Justice. "Luke Homan." January 26, 2019. TV show.

Spignola, Steven. *Staggered Paths: Strange Deaths in the Badger State.* Eau Claire, WI: Badger Wordsmith, 2017.

Spray, Louie. "The Catching of the World Record Musky." Indian Trail Resort. http://www.indiantrailresort.com.

Sutherland, Mary. *Haunted Burlington, Wisconsin.* Charleston, SC: The History Press, 2014.

Swanson, Carl. "A Death at the Eagles Club." Milwaukee Notebook, May 22, 2015. milwaukeenotebook.com.

Tigerman, Kathleen, ed. *Wisconsin Indian Literature: Anthology of Native Voices.* Madison: University of Wisconsin Press, 2006.

Wayland, Tobias. Interview with the author, June 17, 2019.

———. "A Timeline of the Lake Michigan Mothman Sightings So Far." The Singular Fortean Society, June 10, 2017. singularfortean.com.

Wild, Matt. "Return to Haunchyville." *Milwaukee Record*, September 22, 2015.

Wisconsin State Journal. "Bogus Bluff May Still Hide Treasure from Counterfeiters." July 16, 1923.

ABOUT THE AUTHOR

Tea Krulos is a freelance writer and author who was born in Wisconsin and lives in Milwaukee. His previous books include *Heroes in the Night*, *Monster Hunters*, *Apocalypse Any Day Now*, and *American Madness*. He also contributed a chapter to *The Supernatural in Society, Culture, and History*. He frequently gives presentations on paranormal and other unusual topics, is the organizer of the Milwaukee Paranormal Conference and Milwaukee Krampusnacht and leads ghost tours for American Ghost Walks. He writes a weekly column on his website (teakrulos.com) called "Tea's Weird Week."

Visit us at
www.historypress.com
....